Goals and Strategies
for Teaching
Physical Education

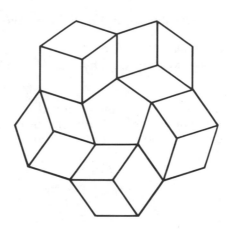

Donald R. Hellison, PhD

Human Kinetics Publishers, Inc.
Champaign, Illinois

Production Director: Karen Morse
Editorial Staff: Stephen C. Jefferies, PhD, Sybelle Timberlake,
  Peg Goyette, Susan Wilmoth, PhD
Photographer: Stephen C. Jefferies
Typesetter: Yvonne Sergent
Text Layout: Lezli Harris
Cover Design and Layout: Jack Davis

Library of Congress Cataloging in Publication Data

Hellison, Donald R., 1938-
    Goals and strategies for teaching physical education.

    Bibliography: p.
    1. Physical education and training—Curricula.
2. Physical education and training—Study and teaching.
3. Problem children—Education.   4. Motivation in
education.   I. Title.
GV363.H45   1984   375.6137   84-15705

ISBN: 0-931250-74-9

Printed in the United States of America

10 9 8 7 6 5 4 3 2 1

Human Kinetics Publishers, Inc.
Box 5076
Champaign, IL 61820

CONTENTS

PREFACE

From my vantage point as a visiting physical education teacher in a number of public schools and diversion/detention programs over the past 15 years, I have formed some impressions about what kids need in physical education. Current trends in society, in the home, and in schools have, in my view, created discipline and motivation problems for teachers and a variety of personal and social problems for young people. My response has been to develop a set of alternative goals for physical education that focus on human needs and values rather than on fitness and sport skill development per se. To try to put these goals into practice, I and a number of my students and colleagues have experimented with many instructional strategies. This book is the product (so far) of the interplay between these ideas and implementation efforts.

The book opens with a brief description of my impressions of the influence of current trends on kids, the program needs that result from these trends, and my alternative goals based on this analysis. From there, the book describes a wide range of strategies that I and about 40 teachers and coaches, with the support of a number of scholars, have found useful in promoting the goals. In this sense, it is a cookbook of gym-tested ideas intended to help students become more personally and socially responsible for their sport and fitness activities, and for their lives. The last chapter cautions the reader that cookbook recipes for human development have limitations.

Throughout the book I talk to you, the teacher, directly— specifying my preferences and thoughts and using references only to acknowledge (when I could sort them out) the ideas of others. I've also tried to repeat my major themes and to approach them in different ways in order to reinforce my perspective. Although the book takes the form of a cookbook, you will need to make professional judgments regarding the extent to which any of the book's suggestions fit your values, your teaching style, and your setting.

In addition to the teachers and scholars mentioned throughout the book, I want to recognize the courageous and creative work of Bill White and Jeff Walsh of Portland, Peter Teppler and Bob Blanchette of Calgary, Alberta, and the remaining members of the Governor's Physical Education Leadership Training Project for High Risk Youth sponsored by the Oregon Governor's Council of Health, Fitness, and Sports: Deta Holcombe, Gayle MacDonald, Lee Jenkins, Tom Hinton, and Jackie Williams. These nine professionals contributed in countless ways to the development of the framework for these goals and strategies.

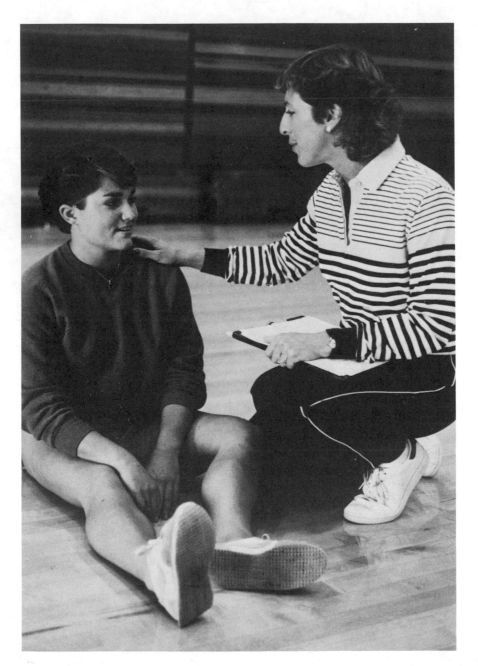

CHAPTER 1

GOALS

Over the past few years, physical education teachers and coaches have expressed increasing concern over discipline and motivation problems in their gyms and on their playing fields. When I ask why they are experiencing so many problems, they often respond with "kids aren't the same anymore," implying that what used to work is no longer effective. I think they are right. Of course, some things that we have always done never have worked well, but kids have changed and so has the world. And so have schools. Kids face more choices today than ever before—from television, the knowledge "explosion," and exposure to different value systems in an increasingly pluralistic society. They are getting less guidance from home (e.g., working mothers and single-parent families) and from neighborhoods that once helped to raise children but are now more mobile and anonymous. We all live in an era of rapid social change and economic uncertainty. In our lifetime the old morality of self-denial, expressions such as "What will the neighbors think?" and "Do it because I said so," and the old work ethic of unlimited economic growth are being challenged by a new value system. There is a concern about the quality of life, an effort to reach higher levels of consciousness, a search for self that is at times obsessive, and a leisure lifestyle identity with overtones of narcissism and new consumerism (e.g., nifty sweat suits, windsurf boards, sailboats, ski equipment). Most kids go to school, but schools are uncertain about their mission in this changing world, and are viewed mainly as babysitters in our society. They are in most cases too large and impersonal, and have failed to involve students in a meaningful and integrated manner.

The results of these trends are mixed. So-called marginal lifestyles are accepted or at least tolerated more than in the past. All of us have more of an opportunity to develop our own uniqueness. A new quality-of-life value orientation appears to be emerging, yet there is also more confusion, insecurity, isolation, and alienation. The teenage suicide rate is up, homicides are increasing, teenage pregnancies are more common despite improved birth control devices, assaults on teachers and other students are more common, and there is more absenteeism from school. Interest in cults has also grown among young people in recent years, suggesting a sense of rootlessness (Cox, 1979). Only drug use seems to have dropped a bit, at least temporarily.

NEEDS AND VALUES

No wonder teachers have been struggling with discipline and motivation problems more than ever before! These trends suggest that if we, as physical education and sport leaders, want to prevent or reduce discipline and motivation problems we had better pay more attention to urgent program needs. Our very survival as professionals is at stake (Is it a good day if the gym hasn't been burned down?), as is our students' ability to cope with and provide leadership for our changing world. Current trends suggest the following needs:

1. We need to improve control in our classes and on our teams. Control is not a very humanistic term, but it is a very real problem. It is difficult to teach and coach if even a few students are out of control. Kids seem to need more attention, probably because of changing home situations and other factors already mentioned, and those who aren't very successful in school often rebel or withdraw. The need for attention and the tendency to rebel or withdraw all translate into control problems. Moreover, as the old morality breaks down, fear and punishment have become less effective. Kids question our methods and resort to physical violence as a way to solve problems. Those who are alienated from the American dream of

success aren't persuaded by the deferred goals (such as diplomas and letter sweaters) that worked in the past.

2. We need to help students make responsible choices. In the areas of personal health and leisure pursuits, as well as everywhere else in their lives, kids are faced with a wider range of options than ever before. Yet those of us in authority are not providing enough guidance in making these choices.

3. We need to help students lead more stable lives. Rapid social change and related trends have led to an increase in confusion, insecurity, isolation, and alienation. Personal stability requires a long-term commitment to personally satisfying activities, thereby giving one's life a day-to-day structure that can be counted on. Personal stability also requires some continuous sense of personal identity, "a consistent set of attitudes that defines 'who I am'. . .and that serves as an anchor in life. . . .People without an integrated and coherent self identity will chronically feel anxiety, insecurity, depression, defensiveness. . .and self-rejection" (Johnson, 1980, p. 12). Social stability requires an infusion of cooperation, caring, and helping, both in small and large groups, toward the development of a better sense of community in our students. The improvement of social stability depends on the development of commitments to others, and on a recognition of the need for support and interdependence in a world that emphasizes the primacy of self.

4. We need to counter the ineffectiveness of schools. Those of us in schools must have a clear mission, and we must find better ways of helping students to be successful. Our classes and teams must also work (and play) toward becoming a family in order to counter the large, impersonal context in many schools.

5. All of these needs must be met without minimizing participation in physical activity, for that, after all, is what we are charged with doing.

Control, responsible choosing, personal and social stability, making schools more effective, teaching physical activities—we need to do all of these things if my interpretation of current trends is accurate. There's nothing very radical here. Traditional human values support all of these concerns in one way or another. Control can act to deny basic freedoms, but sufficient self-control to avoid interfering with the rights of others is a basic human value.

We have more to choose from these days, but sufficient self-responsibility in developing a stable identity and navigating through life is certainly not a new or radical notion. In fact, our heritage emphasizes the individual's freedom and responsibility for life choices. Caring about others is another traditional human value that has been demonstrated in our history of humanitarian concerns. It probably derives from an intrinsic impulse: simply put, we need each other. This value takes on added importance in these times. The notion that we all need meaningful day-to-day activities and a positive sense of personal identity aren't very radical either but, like caring about others, they have taken on added importance in our rapidly changing, less stable world. The importance of teaching physical activities has also received more attention lately, as has the contention that schools need to be made more effective. From a historical perspective, these last two concerns have not enjoyed consistent support, but recent trends have brought both of them into our collective awareness.

GOALS

Traditional physical education goals more or less ignore these current problems. Instead, they focus on exposure to—and occasionally acquisition of—sport and exercise skills, a positive attitude toward an active lifestyle, and related concepts. It is usually assumed (especially by teacher education professors) that students will be under control and that the cooperation and competition integral to physical education programs will automatically embrace social stability. The need for self-responsibility is usually ignored. If my analysis of current trends and resultant needs and values is correct, we can't go on teaching sport and exercise without paying attention to the personal and social instability factors in our society. More specifically, we need to deal directly with the self-control issue while we are teaching students to become involved in our subject matter. And that's just the beginning. Our students also need to learn how to take responsibility for their own learning, for making wise choices, and for developing a meaningful and personally satisfying lifestyle if they are going to make any sense out of the world in which they are growing up. They also need to learn how to cooperate and to support and help one another if they want to achieve any social stability in this rapidly changing world.

Identifying goals such as self-control and self-responsibility which do respond to current trends certainly isn't sufficient to transform an ineffective program into an effective one, but it is a first step. Such goals provide a framework for planning lessons and units and for evaluating student progress. They also give the teacher some guidance in dealing with unplanned incidents (such as fights) so that they become "teachable moments." The second step, the development of strategies to implement these goals, is dependent upon this first step.

To help physical education goals make sense, they are presented throughout this book as developmental levels. This simply means that the goals have been organized into a step-by-step progression of attitudes and behaviors. Students must first show that they can do Level I, Self-Control, to the point that other students' right to learn is protected before Level II, Involvement in the daily motor skill or exercise lesson under teacher supervision, can take place. Level III, Self-Responsibility for working and playing independently, requires that students first demonstrate the ability to become involved under supervision. Level IV, Caring for others, assumes that students have taken charge of their own lives sufficiently to be able to reach out beyond themselves to others.

This progression encompasses both attitudes and behavior, because what we believe and what we intend to do provide the motivation and direction for how we actually behave. Both are necessary if we are to become controlled, involved, responsible, caring human beings. Our actual behavior does not always reveal our intent—for example, we may help someone in order to gain favor with that person or because we feel a sense of obligation to others. Also, our actual behavior often falls short of our intent, yet our attitudes toward doing or not doing something provide the motivation to keep trying. This progression is not fixed, since students are human and don't follow any strictly prescribed progression. However, the levels do provide a framework for planning, responding to specific incidents, and evaluating them, as well as providing a vocabulary (Level I, Level II, etc.) for doing so. A more complete description of the levels follows.

DEVELOPMENTAL LEVELS

LEVEL O: IRRESPONSIBILITY

Level 0 (zero) describes students who are unmotivated and undisciplined; such attitudes and behaviors must be improved if students are to become personally and socially responsible. Students who operate at Level 0 are not motivated to participate in sport and exercise activities; they make excuses and blame others for their behavior, deny personal responsibility for what they do or fail to do, and may feel powerless to change their lives. Their behavior includes discrediting or making fun of other students' involvement as well as interrupting, intimidating, manipulating, and verbally or physically abusing other students and perhaps the physical education teacher. Some students rarely operate at this level but others spend much of their time here.

LEVEL I: SELF-CONTROL

Level I deals with the need for control by requiring students to control their own behavior, thereby shifting responsibility from external forces (e.g., authority figures) to the student. Students at Level I may not participate in the day's activity or show much mastery or improvement, but they are able to control their behavior enough so that they don't interfere with other students' right to learn or the teacher's right to teach or coach. And they do this without being prompted by the teacher very much and without constant supervision. Self-control should be the first goal for all students who are not already under control, for learning cannot take place very effectively without it. Moreover, the more abusive violations of self-control can have damaging effects. Through this process, both self-discipline and the beginning of self-responsibility are encouraged.

LEVEL II: INVOLVEMENT

Level II focuses on the need for physical activity in the program and provides one medium for personal stability by giving students experiences in activities that can become a regular part of their lives. Students at Level II not only show self-control, but are involved in the subject matter. They willingly, even enthusiastically, play, accept challenges, practice motor skills, and train for fitness under the teacher's supervision. This goal is nothing new; it is the goal of most traditional programs. However, it is important to recognize the contribution that involvement makes to society. It enhances our personal stability by giving us meaningful activities that we can engage in on a regular basis.

LEVEL III: SELF-RESPONSIBILITY

Level III emphasizes the need for students to learn to take more responsibility for their choices, and for linking these choices to their own identities. Students at Level III not only show self-control and involvement, but they are also able to work without direct supervision, eventually taking responsibility for their intentions and actions. They can identify their own needs and interests and can begin to plan and execute their own physical education programs. In short, they begin to take responsibility for the direction of their lives and to explore options in the development of "a strong and integrated personal identity" (Johnson, 1980, p. 12). This goal fully rests on the assumption that kids can independently reflect, plan, work, and play if given proper guidance and an appropriate framework. Surely they will need these skills in order to function effectively and productively in our changing world.

LEVEL IV: CARING

Level IV deals with the need for social stability in students' lives by encouraging students to reach out beyond themselves to others—to commit themselves to caring about others. Students at Level IV are motivated to extend their sense of responsibility by cooperating, giving support, showing concern, and helping. Level IV rests on the assumption that students must meet some of their own needs before they can reach out very far or very often to others.

These developmental levels roughly correspond to the values and program needs that I believe underlie many current discipline and motivation problems. Level I, Self-Control, responds to the need for control in our classes and on our teams. Level II, Involvement, responds to the need for physical activity as a central feature of physical education and sport programs and to the need for day-to-day, routinized activities as one aspect of personal stability. Level III, Self-Responsibility, responds to the

need for making responsible choices and to the development of a stable personal identity. Level IV, Caring, responds to the need for making creative, responsible decisions as a group member and to the need for a different approach to schooling. All of these levels also correspond to traditional human values that have received wide support for a long time.

USING STRATEGIES EFFECTIVELY

Clearly identifying these levels provides a framework for planning, evaluating, and responding to unplanned incidents. However, the levels alone do little to ensure that students will progress through them in physical education. In order for this to happen, strategies must be employed which cause students to interact with self-control, involvement, self-responsibility, and caring on a regular basis. The line of research that includes time-on-task studies and academic learning time studies strongly suggests that a key variable in learning is time spent engaged in goal-related activities. If students want to learn to dribble a basketball, they must spend time dribbling (with appropriate feedback, of course). If the goal is self-responsibility, students must spend time practicing being responsible.

Five kinds of general interaction strategies can keep the levels "in front" of students on a regular basis:

1. Teacher Talk. This is what the teacher says to students. One way to have students interact with the levels is to explain those levels, post them, refer to them during a spontaneous act of self-responsibility or caring or, conversely, during uncontrolled behavior.

2. Modeling (Being). This is what the teacher does in the presence of students—it is his or her attitudes and behaviors. Students interact with the levels when the teacher is under control (recognizing different teaching styles ranging from the subdued to the blustery), involved (actively participating whenever possible), responsible, (for example, by keeping promises) and caring (demonstrating concern for each student).

3. Reinforcement. This is any act by the teacher that strengthens a specific attitude or behavior of an individual student. A teacher's praise can be a reinforcer if it is genuine, positive, specific, and appropriate to the situation. Awards can also be reinforcers. So can a formal reward system that gives rewards for meeting certain criteria. So can grades. When attitudes and behaviors which represent the higher developmental levels (levels that are higher than the student's typical attitudes and behaviors) are regularly reinforced in a genuine manner, student interaction with the levels is enhanced.

4. Reflection Time. This refers to time students spend thinking about their attitudes and behaviors in relation to the levels. Such interaction can take place at the end of a class period by asking students to state or record the level (or levels) at which they operated during the period, and the basis for their evaluation.

5. Student Sharing. This happens when students are asked to give their opinions about some aspect of the program. Student sharing results in interaction with the levels by emphasizing the worth of each student's opinion (Level III) and a sense of community in trying to resolve a gray issue (Level IV). In addition, it gives students the opportunity to talk with the teacher about how best to encourage self-control, involvement, self-responsibility, and caring. Opinions about the worth of these values can also be elicited, thereby giving

students the opportunity to evaluate and perhaps even suggest modifications to the developmental level system.

6. Specific Strategies. A sixth group of strategies, simply called Specific Strategies, refers to those activities that increase interaction with a specific level (see Chapters 3 through 6). For example, student contracts may help students operate at Level III; and reciprocal teaching, whereby students pair up and teach each other, may help students to operate at Level IV.

The intention of all of these interaction strategies is to keep self-control, involvement, self-responsibility, and caring "in front" of students so that these qualities eventually become viable choices in their lives both in and outside the gym. Regular interaction with the levels offers students the option of incorporating these values into their lives, but the choice must ultimately rest with them. This intention is supported by the attitudes and behaviors of Level III, Self-Responsibility, which encourages students to take charge of their own lives rather than act as pawns who only respond to external forces (de Charms, 1976).

Of course, individual student differences confound any attempt at implementation. The developmental levels do provide a progression that takes individual differences in attitudes and behaviors into account. However, to be effective the interaction strategies must be used with individuals, small groups, and the whole class as the situation dictates, rather than be indiscriminately applied to everyone.

Perhaps an example of a daily lesson will illustrate how the levels and strategies might work. (The variations, of course, are almost endless.)

Daily Lesson (45 minutes)

Time Allotted	Sample Lesson	Level(s)	Strategy
0-5 minutes	1. Teacher talks about incident in class yesterday, relating the incident to one or more developmental levels.	0, I, II, III, and/or IV	Teacher talk
	2. Students discuss incident.	0, I, II, III, and/or IV	Student sharing

Daily Lesson (45 minutes) (Cont.)

20-30 minutes	3. Daily lesson: exercises, skills, drills, games	II	Modeling, Reinforcement, Specific strategies for Level II (see Chapter 4)
10-15 minutes	4. Independent work or play	III	Reinforcement, Specific strategies for Level III (see Chapter 6)
	5. Helping roles for some students	IV	Reinforcement, Specific strategies for Level IV (see Chapter 6)
	6. Alternative: Extend daily lesson for those who have difficulty working at Level III	II	
	7. Alternative: Counsel Level 0 students	I	Confrontation/ negotiation strategy (see Chapter 3)
3-5 minutes	8. Students report their developmental level for the day, and the basis for their evaluation.	0, I, II, III, and/or IV	Reflection time

CONCLUSION

This chapter has provided an overview of the goals and strategies that I think respond to the trends in our society currently confronting our students. The following chapters describe a wide range of strategies that have been used to help students experience the four developmental levels. Chapter 2 describes the application of teacher talk, modeling, reinforcement, reflection time, and student sharing to all of the levels. Chapters 3 through 6 describe strategies for each developmental level. For example, Chapter 3 deals with Level I, Self-Control Strategies, not only by giving examples of how to use teacher talk, modeling, reinforcement, reflection time, and student sharing, but also by describing strategies specific to self-control that don't fit any of the other categories and have been referred to as Specific Strategies (see p. 10). Finally, Chapters 7 and 8 discuss some limitations to this model and some closing thoughts.

CHAPTER 2

STRATEGIES

This chapter expands the brief description of the five general interaction strategies in Chapter 1 and gives specific examples of how to implement them. The five general interaction strategies can help students interact with each of the four developmental levels as shown in the chart on page 14.

This chapter will help you fill in the blanks in the chart. For example, after reading this chapter you should be able to describe how teacher talk can help students to become more self-controlled, and so on. Specific strategies—those that are unique to each level—are described in Chapters 3 through 6.

INTERACTION STRATEGIES

TEACHER TALK

Everything you and I say when we teach anyone anything is teacher talk. Whether teacher talk facilitates interaction with the levels obviously depends on what we say. It can be used to emphasize the levels and to individually negotiate student problems with the levels. Just using one-liners can help; so can teachable moments during which specific incidents can be related to the

The Five Interaction Strategies

	I. Self-Control	II. Involvement
General Strategies		
Teacher talk		
Modeling (being)		
Reinforcement		
Reflection time		
Student sharing		
Specific Strategies		

	III. Self-Responsibility	IV. Caring
General Strategies		
Teacher talk		
Modeling (being)		
Reinforcement		
Reflection time		
Student sharing		
Specific Strategies		

levels. Designating counseling days or times for talking with individual students during class while the rest play or work gives more opportunities for personalized attention and reduces the before-and-after class rush to hold individual conferences.

Several teachers and coaches teach the levels to their students and use "teachable moments" to hold brief discussions about incidents in class. In fact, this has been one of the most effective uses of the levels. David Lahoz reports a behavioral improvement in his Hispanic alternative-school teenagers just from talking about and posting the levels! Of course, the levels must be expressed in terms that students understand and in ways that appeal to them. For instance, Dan Thompson teaches the levels to his youth sport baseball teams to emphasize their responsibilities to themselves and others. Bill White tells his high school athletic teams that they must learn to operate at Level III rather than depend on him for guidance and motivation, and that the team "veterans" had better be at Level IV because the team needs assistant coaches to be successful. Debbie McFarlane introduces the levels to her elementary school kids this way for Level I: "I am good, can take care of myself, and will respect the rights of others"; for Level IV: "I can help you with that; we can do it together." Deta Holcombe has used tape recorded messages from a "secret agent" to get the levels across to her younger kids. Frank O'Toole gives his middle-school students character descriptions of each level. Here are his descriptions of Levels III and IV:

> Meet Suzie Self-Directed. Suzie is taking charge of herself. She is keenly interested in how her body looks and how it works, so she asked her physical education teacher for information on weight control and heart fitness. She has set a realistic goal of losing 5 pounds and improving her cardiovascular system. Now that she knows the best way to do this, she is working out a daily plan with her teacher. She knows the teacher won't tell her what to do and won't watch her like a hawk to make sure she's doing it. Suzie isn't taking charge of herself for someone else or for high grades. She's doing it for herself and she's learning that that takes courage and determination.

> Meet Harry Caring, who is also self-directed. Unlike Suzie, Harry not only has goals for himself but he gets a real kick out of helping others reach their goals too. Harry is not helping others for the praise he gets from his teacher or to get out of regular physical education class. He genuinely cares about how other people feel and will sometimes leave his own program to show someone else the correct way to lift the weights. Our society needs more people like this.

MODELING (BEING)

What you and I do—who we are when we are with our students—sends loud and clear messages about what's important and how the program is really supposed to work. Often called the "hidden curriculum," modeling is a powerful source of interaction that sometimes runs counter to the planned curriculum. Therefore, one way to get students to interact with the levels is

for the teacher to live the levels as completely as possible. If we want students to show self-control, we must be in control ourselves in our interactions with them. When I "lose it," as I have done so often, I come back and talk about what I should have done. I sometimes wait until the next day, but it is crucial to go back to the incident and work through it with the kids. It also means being involved in the subject matter. This can be conveyed by active participation when appropriate and by attitudes and demeanor. There's no substitute for being "into" activity and our bodies.

Self-responsibility requires that we try very hard to deliver on our promises to students. If I promise a play day on Friday and then forget my promise, I send a message. It also requires taking some responsibility for what goes on in the gym rather than blaming parents, current trends, lack of facilities, and so on. And it means developing a strong and integrated personal identity; kids can sense this in their teachers. Caring doesn't require that every student be loved; some are hard to love! It *does* insist upon loving the act of caring. Being a friend to all the kids isn't necessary (and may be detrimental), but being cold and aloof doesn't convey caring. Teachers are there to help—to facilitate. Sometimes personal needs get in the way (we all have difficulty focusing on helping others when we need help ourselves). Sharing this struggle in general terms with students lets them know that we are human. Being human also requires being able to laugh at oneself. Our results often fall short of our intentions. We need not only to be able to pick ourselves up, to evaluate and try again, but also not to take ourselves too seriously. It's a delicate balance but one that students can begin to learn from our behavior.

REINFORCEMENT

Reinforcement refers to anything the teacher says or does to provide consequences for a student's behavior. For example, when a student swings and misses a ball, the teacher can verbally reinforce the student's effort or the student's level swing, thereby providing a positive consequence for the student even though he missed the ball. You and I reinforce our students all the time, whether we are aware of it or not. Certain kinds of reinforcement cause students to interact with the levels. For example, if a student calls another student a jerk, you could remind that student of her Level O behavior. You might insist that she sit out for awhile. You could award the Most Improved Control award to someone else at the end of the week. You could deduct points that would have earned her some privilege in your program. If a student throws a ball at a target, hitting the target could be reinforcement enough. If he failed to hit the target, you could tell him something that he did right (e.g., his form, his effort). You might give him a Best Effort award or some extra points that could earn him privileges in your program.

TYPES OF REINFORCEMENT

You may be able to discern three kinds of reinforcement from these examples. The first is verbal and nonverbal feedback from the teacher—a comment, a nod, a touch. Second, awards can reinforce and emphasize interaction with the levels. We often give awards for fitness tests and sport skills; why not for the levels? One example of the use of awards is a special program for students who have been suspended from a Portland suburban middle school. The program teaches physical activities and is based on the levels, but it is operated by school counselors and called "Group" since physical education is something most of these kids won't do and have flunked rather consistently. The kids receive certificates of completion at the end of the course. Last year, Group leaders Deta Holcombe and Jan Welle invited me to hand out certificates at a ceremony, and a local newspaper reporter interviewed the kids. It was quite a big deal!

Third, a formal reward system might be necessary to encourage interaction with the levels. Certain criteria which represent the levels can be established and some kind of privilege can be given for those students who meet the criteria. For example, those students who do not interfere with the rights of others during the week and who fully participate in the week's activities earn the privilege of having one free play day a week. Several of us have found that even disruptive students will change their behavior in order to earn some "free" time. Moreover, they will respond to criteria that are considerably different from their usual behavior. For example, we have required students to learn fitness concepts in addition to being under control and involved, and we have required them to fill out contracts and to include some training and practice in their plan as part of their free day (Hellison, 1978). They do it!

Art Seavey devised a scoring system to provide both awards and a reinforcement system for teenagers in an alternative school. At the end of each class period, students who got fully involved, who set goals for themselves, and who helped someone else received a score of 5. Students who got fully involved and who set goals for themselves received a score of 4. Students who got fully involved received a score of 3. Students who "shuffled through" the class with a half-hearted effort received a score of 2. Students who did not participate received a score of 1. Students who interfered with the teacher's job or with other students received a score of zero. The points served as daily awards (and booby prizes) and could also be used to earn privileges in class.

GUIDELINES FOR USING REINFORCEMENT

Reinforcement can be misused if a few guidelines are not observed.

1. Use as little reinforcement as possible to get the job done. The principle of least intervention means that if success in the task is reinforcement enough, don't do anything else. If a word will do, don't use a sentence; overpraise is as ineffective as underpraise. If informal feedback works, don't use awards or rewards. If students won't try something, use reinforcement temporarily to get them involved.

2. Be as positive as you can in giving feedback, awards, or rewards. You may need to say "That's Level 0" or "You'd better sit out awhile," but it's better if you say, "Your control was better today" or "No sitouts for a week—nice going." Award or rewards for attitudes and behavior that represent the levels work better than lists of students who have earned demerits.

3. Be as specific as you can. "Nice job" is not nearly as effective as "Thanks for helping, Joey" or "Good try." If awards are used, Outstanding Student says less than Best Helper. Rewards such as some privilege in class or practice should be clearly connected to level-specific attitudes and behavior.

4. Be honest; your comments must not be contrived just to make some kid feel good. Students can see through that. (They may feel that we care, but they won't believe us if we don't believe ourselves.) Awards and rewards must also be genuine. I've altered criteria for privileges on occasion when I felt that the student was working up to capacity but could not meet the criteria. For example, for a high school kid who could only read at the second-grade level and who had to write a contract to include goals and an individual physical activity plan, I accepted a very rough contract after giving him some individual help. The key here is to make the student feel that he/she did earn the reward.

5. Be gentle and appropriate. If a student who has refused to participate gets involved one day and I respond by yelling out, "Glad to see you're finally with us!" she may quickly return to her seat in the bleachers. Depending on the student and the situation, any praise for a change in behavior may be too much. It may be enough to stop by sometime during the session and ask if everything's okay. A good rule of thumb is to determine whether the student would like some attention for improving in one of the levels. If it would embarrass the student or if it would create uncomfortable expectations by placing pressure on him or her to live up to the praise ("Does this mean I have to be under control every day?"), then the stu-

dent needs to know that the improvement was noticed without a big deal being made about it. On the other hand, students perceive some accomplishments as a big deal and they would enjoy some recognition of their achievement. Research suggests that students from higher socioeconomic areas tend to profit more from challenge and high expectations, whereas students from lower socioeconomic areas need encouragement and praise (Brophy & Evertson, 1976). This is still an individual matter, and it's up to us to know our students well enough to determine what they need.

6. Be aware of the intent of the behavior. Intentions provide motivation and direction for our actions. If intentions are ignored, a student could be reinforced for helping someone when the student's intent is merely to manipulate that person. Since it is very difficult to reinforce intent (it can't be seen), we need to be as sensitive as we can to motives and goals and not allow overt behavior to overshadow intentions. One way to do this is to ask students individually about their intentions in relation to a particular behavior and to verbally reinforce intentions that reflect the developmental levels.

GRADES AS REINFORCEMENT

Grades, if they are part of your program, provide students with yet another type of reinforcement, causing students to interact with the teacher's evaluation process and product. If grades are to help students interact with the levels in a positive way, the process of grading must be based on improvement; that is, students must be evaluated on an individual basis from where they are with respect to their self-control, involvement, self-responsibility, and caring upon entering the program. Evaluation of student progress in each of the levels can be built into the grading system in a number of ways. The attendance book provides a record of involvement—of attendance and participation—and it is a convenient place to record incidents of lapses in self-control, of participation in independent activities, and of helping roles in class. One way to convert these records into grades is to award a "C" to those students who show both self-control and participation for a certain number of days in the grading period, for example 80%. To earn a "B", students would have to demonstrate some independent behavior in addition to meeting the criteria. Earning an "A" would require helping behavior in addition to self-control, involvement, and self-responsibility. A variation of this grading system begins with self-control and involvement as the only criteria for an "A", adds self-responsibility and helping as the year progresses, and ends with students developing their own grading system.

Gayle MacDonald, Tom Hinton, and Jeff Walsh have used a "report card" for students to grade their own behavior at each level, to be followed by the teacher's grade of the same behaviors. Some excerpts from their report card include the following:

Level	Behavior	Self-Grade	Teacher Grade
I	Does not call others names		
I	Controls temper		
I	Does not disrupt class		
II	On time to class		
II	Tries new activities		
II	Listens to instructions		
III	Makes and follows contract		
III	Writes in journal every day		
IV	Shares equipment		
IV	Treats others kindly		
IV	Shows good sportsmanship		

Another variation involves basing some percentage of the grade on an evaluation of each level. This system would permit the teacher to emphasize skill and fitness (Level II) by giving them more weight, but it requires more computation. Finally, self-control and involvement could be coupled with some choice of grading criteria to emphasize self-responsibility. Hugh Twa has his students select from a range of evaluation procedures such as tournament results, skill and fitness tests, an officiating exam, and knowledge tests. Hugh says that this system permits the "Joe Jock" types to select more skill-oriented procedures while permitting "Sam Student" types to choose written exams. However, he requires all students to select several evaluation procedures so that they cannot specialize completely. Gary Kuney has implemented a similar procedure with his elementary school classes. He offers nine options including book reports, effort, skill improvement, observing safety rules, participation in an exercise physiology lab, and a rules test. Students are required to do four of these options for their grade. Whatever grading system is used, that system should reflect the teacher's goals, in this case the developmental levels.

REFLECTION TIME

Some of the interaction with the levels ought to take place in the students' head. They need to think about their attitudes and behavior in relation to levels and ask themselves: "What level am I operating at today?" Such reflection can lead to the development of conscience, because it strengthens the concept that behavior is not complete until the student reflects upon it and upon its effects on self and others.

The final minutes of class or practice can be set aside for reflection time. Just asking students to respond to what level they were at during class may be enough. Or use specific questions: Did they hurt anyone (Level I)? Did they learn anything (Level II)? Did they work well without direct supervision (Level III)? Did they help anyone (Level IV)? This can be done verbally or by requiring students to make an entry in their journal, fill out a check list, or grade their behavior in relation to the levels.

My alternative-school students are required to make a journal entry at the end of each class period, which describes what level they were at that day and what they did or tried to do to earn that level. I then read their entries and write in their journals what I thought they earned and why. Because they are at different levels at different times during the period, students tend to give themselves an "average level" for the day. For example, a little bit of Level 0 (zero), mostly Level II, and some Level IV might equal Level II plus. This scoring system (or quasi-system) seems to work well, so I am now using it and teaching it to new students. Journals are time-consuming with large classes, so Jeff Walsh has his students tell him what level they were at as they leave the gym. If he disagrees, he stops them, and they negotiate. I've tried this approach but have required students to give me a brief reason for the level they selected. One student said: "I was at Level II but you ought to give me a Level III for saying I was a II!" She was being cute, of course, but her response showed some reflection and understanding of the levels.

Jackie Williams has her emotionally handicapped teenagers grade themselves on each level. Kim Weaver requires her emotionally handicapped children to fill out a check list which includes fought, sat out, got angry, was happy, cooperated. Pam Yoder has her high school students fill out a check list with these categories: was on time, tried my best, had a good attitude toward others.

Designating specific time for counseling as suggested earlier— that is, counseling one student at a time while the rest work or play—can also provide opportunities for students to reflect on their awareness (Did I think of that alternative before acting?), intentions (What was my motive?), and behaviors (What did I do?).

STUDENT SHARING

Student sharing takes place every time we ask students for their group opinion about what is (or is not) going on or what ought to go on in our program. If some of their suggestions are adopted or adapted, they will begin to feel some ownership in the program. Ownership leads to interaction with Level III by emphasizing the worth of each person's opinion. If even a 5-minute group discussion is held once a week, a sense of community may begin to develop as students exchange ideas, deal with conflicts, and reach consensus. All of these emphasize Level IV activities.

The questions that we ask the group can also encourage interaction with the levels. The following are sample questions for each level. Level I: How can we protect the rights of everyone in here? What should the rules be? What should the consequences be? What about some sportsmanship guidelines? Safety procedures? Level II: What activities are you most interested in learning? How can we make learning and fitness playful? Level III:

How can we individualize this program? Level IV: What qualifications should we use for becoming a teaching assistant? Could we do a better job of helping each other in here?

ANALYSIS OF THE STRATEGIES

I have called these five groups of ideas *general interaction strategies*. Together with another category—those strategies specific to a particular level that don't fit anywhere else—they form the basis for implementing the developmental levels (or goals). If you go back to the chart on page 14, you should be able to fill in the blanks of the chart (sneaking another look at this chapter is permissible). When you finish, it might look like this:

General Interaction Strategies

	I. Self-Control	II. Involvement
Teacher talk	Teach Level I to students with examples from class.	Teach Level II to students with examples from class.
Modeling (being)	Don't blow up!	Get involved with students in your lesson.
Reinforcement	Praise students for being under control without prompts.	If necessary, reward students to get them involved.
Reflection time	Require students to reflect on the extent of their self-control in class that day.	Require students to reflect on the extent of their involvement in class that day.
Student sharing	Ask students how the class can do a better job of protecting everyone's rights.	Ask students what they want to learn.
Specific strategies	See Chapter 3	See Chapter 4

	III. Self-Responsibility	IV. Caring
Teacher talk	Teach Level III to students with examples from class.	Teach Level IV to students with examples from class.

General Interaction Strategies (Cont.)

Modeling	Keep your promises to students.	Be a caring teacher.
Reinforcement	Give awards for independent work.	Praise students (gently and appropriately) who help others.
Reflection time	Require students to reflect on the extent of their responsible, self-directed behavior in class that day.	Require students to reflect on the extent that they helped or supported others.
Student sharing	Ask students if they want time to work independently.	Ask students whether they would like a more supportive environment in class.
Specific strategies	See Chapter 5	See Chapter 6

Wolfgang and Glickman (1980, pp. 11-19) have conceptualized a continuum of strategies ranging from nonintervention on one end to intervention on the other with interaction as the middle range. For example, modeling (being) is a nonintervention strategy, according to Wolfgang and Glickman, because such teacher behavior provides a "facilitative environment" for student growth. Student sharing is categorized as an interaction strategy, because students are encouraged to interact with the teacher within a specified framework (the levels). Reinforcement, when it appears as a formal reward system, is seen by Wolfgang and Glickman as an interventionist strategy because the goal is to change behavior by controlling the environment. Strategies that occupy the nonintervention end of the continuum place more faith in students' ability to make changes in their lives, whereas strategies at the intervention end rely on teacher intervention to make changes. The strategies that have been described so far and those that will be described in the next four chapters come from all points on the nonintervention/interaction/intervention continuum. However, the intent of all strategies is to keep students interacting with the developmental levels, not only to improve their here-and-now discipline and motivation but, more importantly, so that the attitudes and behaviors represented by the levels become viable choices outside the gym and in later life. In this sense, then, they are all interaction strategies.

CURRICULUM CONSIDERATIONS

Curriculum refers to the selection and organization of subject matter. Since our subject matter is physical activity, our curriculum consists of selected activities arranged in a sequence and often packaged in 1- to 3-week units. You may be uncomfortable about changing your curriculum, or you may be stuck with teaching soccer in the fall in a 3-week unit. Or your teaching style may be spontaneous enough that fattening your "bag of tricks" with some of these strategies will be sufficient. On the other hand, you may be willing to make some drastic changes in your practice schedule, or you may run a "self-contained" gym with full responsibility for what to teach, for how long, and with the help of only an outdated, vague curriculum guide. Or you may need to create a new structure to make any changes.

INFUSING THE STRATEGIES
INTO YOUR CURRENT CURRICULUM

The most conservative approach, and one that will risk the least, is to retain your current schedule and to fit into it some changes in what you say, what you do, what you reinforce, and what your students experience, in addition to your usual plan. For example, you could talk about and post the awareness levels. You could consciously praise students who exhibit responsible and caring behavior. You might even institute some kind of award system on a daily or weekly basis. You could end class or practice with some of the self-control strategies described in Chapter 3. And so on. To implement this conservative approach, you will need to select those strategies that will best help your students interact with the developmental levels and then infuse those strategies into your current curriculum.

CHANGING YOUR ACTIVITIES

If you want to go a step further and change your curriculum, two choices are open to you. First, you may wish to substitute activities that by their nature emphasize one or more of the levels for some of your current activities. For example, contact sports and combative activities emphasize the need for Level I, Self-Control. Level III, Self-Responsibility, can be emphasized through fitness activities by giving students the task of doing as many repetitions as they can, of progressing at their own rate, or of setting their own fitness goals. Volleyball, which encourages each team to cooperate by using all three hits each time the ball comes over the net, can be used to emphasize Level IV, Caring; and so on.

CHANGING YOUR CURRICULUM DESIGN

Second, you may wish to change your daily, weekly, or yearly curriculum design so that the developmental levels become your organizing centers rather than sport and exercise activities. This kind of change will require more of an overhaul of your program than simply "sneaking" some interaction strategies into what you now do. One advantage is that such changes force you to do something with the levels, whereas infusing the strategies into what you now do relies on your daily energy and courage to do the necessary infusing. Pages 10 and 11 contain an example of a daily curricular design. Following are examples of weekly and yearly curriculum designs. Each can be modified to suit your situation.

Weekly Curriculum Design*

Day	Activity	Level	Strategy
Mon/Wed	Activity (usual unit)	II	see Chap. 4
Tues/Thurs	Individual fitness programs or contracts	III	see Chap. 5
Friday	Cooperative games	IV	see Chap. 6

*In this design, different days of the week are focused on a specific developmental level.

Yearly Curriculum Design*

Season	Level	Strategies
Fall	I, II	see Chaps. 2-4
Winter	I, II, III	see Chaps. 2-5
Spring	I, II, III, IV	see Chaps. 2-6

*In this design, developmental levels (goals) are added as the year progresses so that the teacher is not faced with trying to implement all four levels at once.

The levels and instructional strategies in this book need not be restricted to physical education. Indeed, if we really want our students to interact with the levels, all teachers, counselors, and parents need to become involved. One middle school in Portland uses the levels in classrooms, in the halls, and on the playgrounds, thanks to Jeff Walsh's implementation in physical education 3 years before the all-school adoption. Counselors and teachers of other subjects in a number of schools have found the levels and the interaction strategies useful.

INDIVIDUALIZATION

So far, two major concepts have provided the basis for this approach to teaching and coaching. First, the goals are developmental in nature. Second, the strategies depend on interaction in order to be effective. A third concept, that of individualization, is also crucial to implementation and has been implied all along. Much lip service has been paid to this concept in recent years as a result of our changing values as described earlier. I have been responsible for some of this lip service myself! Jumping from rhetoric to reality is no easy task, but I see no way around facing the variety of skills, motivational levels, values, socioeconomic backgrounds, and racial and ethnic groups we see in our gyms. Students do indeed march to different drummers despite the pressure of the socialization process and each student's need for approval, and current trends have clearly stepped up the drumming.

The developmental levels provide a framework, but individualization requires a recognition that each student begins at a different place within this framework and that encouragement to progress from that point is crucial to individual student success. For one kid, just getting to some consistent Level I behavior is a monumental chore; participation in the activity program will have to wait. For another, the levels are no problem until he is asked to take his own time to help someone. The developmental levels aren't meant to provide an automatic progression that kids can be lockstepped through. People don't work that way! On the other hand, they *are* intended to provide interested physical education and sport leaders with some guidance; treating students as individuals without some kind of framework trusts the process of development to intuition, chance, or the vagaries of external pressure (i.e., socialization).

The interaction strategies provide some ways of helping students progress through the levels, but they aren't meant to be used indiscriminately. Any strategy in this book can have a positive, neutral, or negative effect on students, depending on the sensitivity with which it is implemented. Being gentle and appropriate, as suggested for reinforcement strategies, may be a reasonable guideline in many cases, but it is also true that some students must be confronted directly in order for interaction to occur. There is no substitute for sizing up your students, both individually and as a group, before implementing anything! Some examples: Teacher talk provides an opportunity to emphasize and explain the levels, but all kids don't need all the levels emphasized and explained. If reinforcement is done in accordance with the principle of least intervention, some kids will need more intervention than others. Since reinforcement is specific, some will need reinforcement for improvement in one level, some another. Student sharing provides an opportunity for students to express their opinions, yet some students may need to develop talking and listening skills before they can effectively engage in student sharing activities. Specific strategies also need to pay attention to the individual. The talking bench, a self-control strategy described in Chapter 3, works quite well with kids who want to participate in the activities of the day, but not with those who don't care or who would rather sit out. Written contracts, described in Chapter 5, aren't very effective with kids who can't read and write! And so on.

In addition, the concept of interaction itself requires some individualization. A teachable moment or critical incident may profoundly affect one student while others who were there remain untouched. Even if interaction is held constant, though it never can be, effects on individual students will differ.

Finally, we need to use the levels and strategies in our own ways, to integrate them with our values and teaching style, to fit them to our setting and students, to pick and choose, and to delete and modify as we deem necessary. In short, the concept of individualization also applies to us.

WHAT'S NEXT?

By this time, you should begin to understand how the five general interaction strategies can help students experience the four developmental levels. Each of the next four chapters focuses on one of the developmental levels. The level is described in some detail, and examples of the five general interaction strategies are given. In addition, specific strategies for each level which do not fit any of the five general strategy categories are described in some detail.

CHAPTER 3

SELF-CONTROL
STRATEGIES (LEVEL I)

Maintaining order heads the list of teacher concerns in most recent polls. While good class or team control does not ensure that learning is taking place, if even a few students are out of control the whole learning process is interrupted, not to mention its effect on the teacher's stress level. Control is a first order of business: without it, other goals are difficult to pursue.

Too often, control is interpreted as external pressure to force student compliance with program rules and regulations. External force encourages students to duck personal responsibility for their behavior. The issue becomes "What can I get away with?" Such an attitude only intensifies the need for control in our society in general and in any specific setting in which the authority figures aren't powerful enough to exert external force. As a nation we have rather consistently supported the concept of individual responsibility for controlling the excesses of one's own behavior. It is this value which forms the basis for the first developmental level.

DEVELOPMENTAL LEVEL I

Self-control refers to the ability and willingness of students to exert control over their actions to the point that the rights of others are protected. Respect for the rights of others is perhaps the least any of us can do for each other; it is a nonnegotiable, minimal standard of conduct which emphasizes personal responsibility as opposed to external control by some authority. Behaviors which require self-control include: verbal abuse such as name calling or making fun of someone; physical abuse such as starting a fight or pushing someone; intimidation such as taking someone's turn or space or equipment; manipulation such as using someone for personal gain; cheating in games; and distracting either the teacher or other students from assigned tasks. A student who operates at Level I may not be personally productive or especially helpful to others, but the intent and behavior of self-control marks the beginning of both self-responsibility and an ethical lifestyle.

The point at which one person's rights end and another's begin is sometimes difficult to determine. Most acts affect others at least indirectly—for example, choosing to be obese increases the chances that one's own children will be obese—so that very little of what we do has a purely personal consequence. Yet in most of my experiences with students, both the right and the interference are quite obvious. A fight may be the product of two or more students mutually interfering with each other's rights, but often one student has simply been trying to protect him/herself.

Lack of self-control may stem from failure in school or with peers, from "street" values which emphasize a survival-of-the-fittest perspective, or from genetic or behavioral disorders. Attitudes and behavior may be deeply rooted and not amenable to the following strategies. In that case, counseling or special help is necessary. My rule of thumb is that if a student is at least making some progress toward self-control, even though he/she may not be participating in other ways or showing other kinds of responsibility, I'll stick with the student. If I don't see any progress and have exhausted my strategies (and myself), I'll use referral as a last resort. It is very important to have an effective referral system at your school or in your program; if you don't, you've got to lobby for one or develop your own. The use of consultants and referral systems in schools is described in some detail by Joncs and Jones (1981, pp. 315-324), and Alschuler (1980) offers a provocative alternative to referral systems.

INTERACTION STRATEGIES

TEACHER TALK

Teacher talk provides an excellent opportunity to emphasize the importance of self-control and to explain what it is and how it works, thereby encouraging students to interact with this beginning step toward responsibility for self and others. In this way, teacher talk can help to prevent disruptive behavior from occurring as well as to reduce discipline problems. Here are some teacher talk strategies that have been useful in emphasizing and explaining Level I:

THE FIRST RULE: SELF-CONTROL

One strategy involves conveying to students that the first rule is not to interfere with others' rights. Choices include telling them as a group (perhaps repeatedly), posting the first rule, or telling only those who have broken the rule. It depends on one's style, the setting, and the kids. The major point is that among the welter of school, gym, and team rules, this is the most important one. I have said, "Walking across the gym floor in high heel shoes is not okay, but if you really want my attention, break the first rule."

REVIEW AND PRIORITIZE RULES

It might be a good idea to review all the rules to see if they are really necessary, or at least to prioritize them. Gayle MacDonald hands out these rules to her inner-city high school students:

1. Bottomline Rule #1: You cannot interfere with others' right to learn or participate, or with my right to teach.

2. Bottomline Rule #2: You cannot jeopardize the safety of yourself or another classmate.

3. Keep an open mind.

4. To participate you must be dressed down in tennis shoes and clothes in which you can move. You can wear shorts, sweats, jeans, leotard, etc., but it is NOT OK to wear your school clothes in PE.

5. When you forget your clothes you will come and tell me you're here, then go back to the locker room for the rest of the period. ("The washing machine broke down" or any other handy excuse for forgetting your clothes won't work on me.)

6. Stay in the locker room until the passing bell rings.

7. If you're late, come in quietly without talking and sit down.

8. If you cannot participate for a medical reason, bring me a note from your parents or doctor and I will give you another assignment. The excuse should indicate how long you will be out.

TEACH THE LEVELS

Another approach is to teach, or post, the levels to students as described in Chapter 1. Since self-control is Level I, its importance is solidly established as a prerequisite to participation. It can be emphasized with a sense of humor ("What a Level Zero Day! Did somebody spike the water?"), by being vulnerable ("I blew it—no self-control today"), and by a willingness to dialog ("Looked like Level Zero to me—What do you think?").

POINT OUT NEGATIVE CONSEQUENCES

One-liners or a brief sentence to point out negative consequences of specific actions can help students learn the importance of self-control. Barb Pallari tells her alternative-school teenagers that the source of much of their trouble is lack of self-control. Their peers, whose rights are violated, tend to "come down on them" and so do people in authority. Self-control makes sense because it reduces their problems. Every time we have to interrupt what we are saying to prompt students to pay attention, others who aren't involved must wait. Many jokes are at the expense of other students. Not trying often ruins the game for others. And so on. Sharing our feelings and perceptions with individual students emphasizes this point. I tell them how I feel about what they are doing and how it affects me. I've found these subjective sharing sessions to be at least as powerful as objective statements about behavior, causes, and consequences.

TRANSFER OUTSIDE THE GYM

Talking briefly about the transfer of self-control outside class or practice might help. One-liners can be worked into the lesson or in response to a particular situation. For example: "Families, neighborhoods, even cities work the same way" or "It's like being a member of a team. Your family is a team, like it or not. What other teams do you belong to?" or "Blaming others gets to be a habit both in here and elsewhere in your life." Bill White posts a sign that reads, "It's your trip" and that shows an age line from 0 to 70 with an "X" at his students' age (14-18). He refers to the sign often. For example, when a student interrupts him by talking loudly, Bill talks about how self-control plays a part in whether people choose you for a job or as a friend later in life.

A CONFRONTATION/NEGOTIATION PROCESS

Teacher talk can also be used to negotiate with students who interfere with the rights of others in the program. In this way, teacher talk can help reduce problems. One strategy that has good support, both in the literature and in my experience, is a confrontation/negotiation process (Glasser, 1965, 1974; Raffini, 1980, pp. 107-141) that can help to deal with students or on the teacher's right to teach. If there is some uncertainty that the students did break the "first rule"—for example, the student may have been using some form of self-protection—that obviously needs to be dealt with first. In either case the dialog process follows the same steps:

1. Identify both the student's behavior and the "first rule";

2. Listen to the student's response;

3. Provide a transition from the student's description to making a plan;

4. Help the student make a plan to change the behavior if necessary;

5. Follow up to be certain that the student carries out the plan;

6. Make a new plan if the first one didn't work, that is, if the behavior continues.

The main guideline in trying to achieve a Level I attitude and behavior is to require students to participate in the process. The teacher cannot play a police role. The student must be involved at least to some extent in the decision-making.

If the student storms out, welcome to the club! I usually let him/her cool off, *then* start the negotiation process. It may have to wait until the next day. In a school situation I also give the student no credit for the day—to reinforce the irresponsibility involved in walking out. Of course that too is negotiable. If the student won't talk, skip step 2 and offer a couple of options. If silence still prevails, choose one of the options for the student. If the student fails to carry out the selected plan, sit down again and start over but don't try the same plan again (it didn't work). If the student totally denies doing what was clearly observed (a common occurrence in some settings in which I've worked), say "That's not a choice" and go right on with the process, or place the burden on the student to "prove" innocence. If the student claims ignorance of the first rule, a brief discussion of the "ignorance is no excuse" policy of other authorities in society might help.

The student's viewpoint and/or the dialog with the student may make it clear that no further action is necessary. If so, that's the end of it; there is no need to go on to the next steps. It is important, however, that the student be involved in this decision rather than looking to the teacher as judge and jury.

To make a transition from listening to planning, it may be useful to call the student's attention to the first rule again to divert attention from the long list of excuses for the behavior. A one-liner might help, for example: "Your behavior is all you can control" or "If what you did had worked for you we wouldn't be discussing all this now" or "Sometimes I wish the world were different too" or "My job is to be responsible for all of you."

The ideal situation has the student making a plan. In real life, the teacher may have to lend a hand and therefore must have some options available. The key is to get the student involved at least to some extent in *self*-control. If the student admits breaking the first rule, that may be enough the first time around; after all, that does show some responsibility. Some options are sitting out, staying away from some individuals, playing and working alone such as by using a ball and wall, working out the problem with other involved students, some kind of reinforcement system, and so on.

Sometimes asking a slightly different question can help the student to become involved in the planning process. For example, a student who tends to have emotional outbursts might be asked, "What can you do when you're about to fly off the handle to reduce the problem for all of us?" He might suggest going to a corner of the gym to punch and kick a crash pad, or the teacher might suggest something similar.

To follow up, some symbols in the attendance book or on a clipboard may help to keep track of the various plans that are supposed to be under way. The teacher's style, setting, and students may dictate some modifications of this process. In most cases, the steps overlap and take place very informally. In all cases, however, there must be time for a one-on-one conference, either during class time or by appointment.

MODELING

Strategies based on modeling (being) may also help students to interact with Level I.

MODELING SELF-CONTROL

Teachers model self-control skills every time they respond to a student's misbehavior. When I pushed a kid against the lockers

after he set fire to an emotionally handicapped classmate's shirt, I was setting a poor example of self-control for that student and others standing around. Teachers aren't held to a "first rule" by someone else, at least not to the extent that students can be (although trends in lawsuits could change this). Therefore, they must control their own behavior. The extent to which they do sends a message to students about the importance of self-control in their own lives. Actually, they don't send the message—they are the message! When I do lose control, I talk to my students about it. They need to know that I'm human too. Besides, such talks help them to focus on self-control.

MODELING VERBAL "TEASES"

Teachers can also model such things as the difference between a verbal putdown and a verbal "tease" or joke. The key, of course, is whether the target of our remark enjoys the comment and appreciates the attention or whether he/she is hurt or offended. Calling a student a loser, for example, could work either way. It is up to teachers to be sensitive enough to know when to say what. Just by doing it appropriately can teach kids the difference. (The differences can also be discussed to drive the point home.)

MODELING SELF-CONTROL WHILE PLAYING

With a small class or some kind of station rotation, playing with students occasionally will give the teacher lots of opportunities to model self-control (as in the paragraphs above).

REINFORCEMENT

Reinforcement can help to promote self-control as long the reinforcement is not reduced to a form of external pressure to force compliance with program rules. The principle of least intervention must be used, and the goal must be for the student to internalize or personally "own" his/her attitudes and behaviors.

PRAISE

One kind of reinforcement which always makes sense is to genuinely and specifically praise students as a group and individually for showing unusually good self-control, for doing their negotiated plan, or for making progress toward self-control. Progress is especially important to emphasize; it often goes unnoticed if the positive behavior continues. For example, a kid who reduces his or her outbursts from six a day to four should be praised for this improvement. In organized sport on the field, paying attention to the number of outbursts of students who have control problems helps the teacher to focus on improvement. For it to work, the praise must be genuine (the teacher must believe it) and specific (rather than "nice job," say what was nice about it). Be careful not to overload students with how good things are; such reinforcement tends to lose its meaning after a while.

AWARDS

Giving awards for improved self-control in various units or activities on a regular basis helps to keep students aware of the importance of this level, such as the "Didn't step on anyone's gym shoes this week" award.

REWARDS

A reward system may be necessary to begin the self-control process. I have been in situations in which nothing else seemed to work (including all of the above strategies!). Students often learn to control their behavior when a payoff is involved. One approach is to carefully define the appropriate behavior necessary to earn a "clean day" (i.e., a day free of "first rule" infractions) and to offer some reward to those students who accumulate several "clean days" in a row. The number can depend on how much may be reasonably expected from at least a few students in order to get started. The reward I've used is a free-play day or independent work-play day (with whatever restrictions deemed necessary) for those who meet the requirements. As soon as one student is able to do what he/she wants while others have to be teacher directed, there is usually a big effort by other students to earn "clean days." Jeff Walsh's students earn the right to be on "student time," which means time to work and play in activities in which they have some choice. Students who have not demonstrated self-control remain on "teacher time," which means that they must stay with Jeff doing teacher-planned activities.

A more informal way to do this involves giving everyone a "free" day every week (e.g., on Friday) with the stipulation that students who can't demonstrate sufficient self-control will have to join a group under the teacher's supervision.

Gary Kuney uses a different reward system; he gives points to students who report someone who makes a "kill statement" (e.g., "you jerk") and takes points away from those who make the kill statements. Thirty-five points earn an after-school movie and popcorn at the end of the year. Also, if he hears a "kill statement," the offending student is required to say three positive things to the victim. Although such a system appears to encourage tattling (ratting, finking), Gary says that it works to reduce Level Zero behavior.

REFLECTION TIME

Reflection time provides an opportunity for self-evaluation at the end of class periods or practices, thereby encouraging students to think about the extent of their self-control that day.

SELF-EVALUATION

I've had students make brief journal entries at the end of one or more periods each week. Sometimes I have required them to reflect on their self-control that day. It doesn't take much class time, but reading and responding to the journal entries is time consuming. An approach taken from the values clarification literature is to ask students for one word that represents their behavior that day. They can sit in a circle and say their word when it is their turn. Another is to give students a list of behaviors and have them check those they did that day.

COUNSELING DAYS

Another way to encourage reflection is to schedule a counseling day or time every 2 weeks or so. Counseling days involve talking individually to some student while the rest of the class plays or (if possible) is engaged in some independent activity. Students must be made aware that the major purpose of this day is to talk—hence, no moans or groans when they are pulled out of a game. Without counseling days scheduled in as part of the program, such interactions are left to chance, to before and after class or practice, or to crises. Counseling day talks provide opportunities for teacher talk (dialog) and for reinforcement as well as reflections on self-control and other things that week.

STUDENT SHARING

Student sharing can be used to discuss specific types of behavior that clearly interfere with the rights of others, thereby involving students in the development of an operational definition of self-control.

INCREASING STUDENT AWARENESS

Student sharing can be used effectively to discuss possible consequences for violations of established self-control rules. This process serves as a preventive technique by elevating student awareness of consequences. It also lends some support for consequences that might be suggested in the confrontation/negotiation process (see pp. 37-39).

I've used the above ideas in the first 5 minutes of class or at the end of class periodically as a substitute for self-reflection time. I've found that kids can readily identify disruptive behavior and that, if anything, the consequences they suggest are too punitive—and this from so-called problem teenagers.

STUDENT "JURIES"

Some teachers have had success in involving their students in group decisions about specific incidents. This requires a special touch on the part of the teacher so that the involved student gets help rather than grief (although sometimes a little grief helps!).

SPECIFIC STRATEGIES

Strategies specific to Level I can be used as needed to help students learn better self-control. Each of the following strategies can be implemented quite easily as an integral part of an activity program. The first three strategies are designed to help students solve their own problems.

THE "TALKING BENCH"

The talking bench (Horrocks, 1978) is not a bench that reprimands students! Instead, it refers to a bench or place to which two students who are having an argument can be sent to resolve the problem. They will need to agree on how it started

and that it is over and report back before returning to the activity. This approach works especially well if the involved students *want* to get back into the activity. The major advantage is to shift responsibility for solving problems of rights (who is right and/or whose rights are being violated) from the teacher (as the great arbiter in the sky) to the students. Jeff Walsh requires his middle-school students to make up the time they missed after school (reinforcement). One teacher apparently tapes two lines on the floor to provide the "appropriate" distance between students (Jones & Jones, 1981, p. 218). Often students will need assistance in this process. Kim Weaver lets her emotionally handicapped kids try to work it out, then she joins them to help.

SELF-OFFICIATING

Another experience that requires students to control their behavior is officiating their own games—that is, requiring them to call their own fouls and so on. A variation involves rewarding students who call their own violations in games that are teacher-officiated by doubling the penalty if the official calls a violation alone or first (Harris et al., 1982). Organized sport tends to discourage self-control by placing responsibility for rule infractions on officials. Somehow, coaches need to help students assume more responsibility for controlling their own behavior. Practice in self-officiating provides such opportunities.

THE EMERGENCY PLAN

A related strategy is the emergency plan (thanks to Rudy Benton). Before playing a game or holding class, ask students to decide how they will handle disputes about rules, infractions, personality conflicts, and so on should these arise. For example, they could require those arguing to sit out for 5 minutes; they could flip a coin (if applicable); they could hear both sides and take a vote, and so on. Again, students are engaged in controlling their own behavior.

A SPECIAL STATION

Kim Weaver has a special station to which her emotionally handicapped youngsters can retreat when they feel themselves losing control. The station is equipped with one set of boxing gloves and a crash pad, and everyone is instructed on proper punching techniques early in the year. Many of these kids just can't fully control their emotional outbursts, but they can begin to identify early signs that they are losing control and then do something about it.

PARTICIPATING IN CONTACT SPORTS

Contact sports and activities require self-control in order to participate. I use volleyball a lot just because there is a net between teams! However, participation in contact sports can be used as a reward for self-control. I've used this approach particularly with combative activities such as karate and boxing. Everyone can engage in skill and fitness activities related to combatives, but only those who show self-control in drills can advance to a semi-contact situation and eventually to a contact session. Drills can be executed alone against wall mats or other soft equipment, in front of a mirror, or just by shadow sparring. If students show self-control in these drills, they can work with a partner, hitting each other's hands. If they show control here, they can try semi-contact by sparring using the nondominant hand only, or with a line between partners, or by going half speed. The last step is contact which still requires self-control so that punches and kicks are "pulled" and that no one cranks up the intensity beyond three-quarter speed, especially if embarrassed by a punch or kick that scores.

CURRICULUM CONSIDERATIONS

If emphasizing Level I makes sense to you, you need to evaluate both what is going on (and not going on) in your current program before embarking on a plan to introduce Level I interaction strategies to your students. The chart in Chapter 2 can be helpful in these tasks, but you may want to do a more detailed analysis. The first level of analysis involves identifying the disruptive behavior occurring in your program. How many times do you have to remind or prompt students to do something or refrain from doing something?

  Do one or two behaviors seem to require more prompts? What percent of your students are disruptive? How often? What specific incidents happened last week (or month) and why? Any information you can gather on the extent and quality of your students' self-control will help you to determine how many, if any, Level I strategies to implement. A second level of analysis involves looking at the long-range need for preventing self-control problems. If your students don't need prompts and aren't involved in disruptive activities, or even if they are, you may sense the need for

Match-Ups

Strategy	Purpose
Teacher talk:	
The first rule	Prevention of disruptive behavior
Teaching the levels	Prevention of disruptive behavior
The negotiation/ confrontation process	Deal with individual problems
Modeling (being):	
Self-control of the teacher	Prevention of disruptive behavior
Reinforcement:	
Praise for improved self-control	Deal with individual problems
Reward system	Discourage disruptive behavior
Reflection time:	
Counseling days	Deal with individual problems
Student sharing:	
Suggesting consequences for misbehavior	Discourage disruptive behavior
Specific activities:	
The talking bench	Resolve arguments
Self-officiating	Resolve arguments

prevention strategies to head off future problems. Once you have done these analyses—and they can be accomplished very quickly and informally—it is time to review the interaction strategies to identify those that meet your specific needs. Page 47 contains some sample match-ups. (You can make your own.)

Self-control cannot be planned in quite the same way as the other levels. Without control, nothing else will work very well. Involvement in sport and exercise, independent activity, cooperation and helping—all depend at least to some extent on everyone's self-control. Therefore, every day is self-control day. Or, if everything is under control, no days are self-control days, unless of course you decide to implement some prevention strategies to keep certain things under control, or you want students to leave your program with an appreciation for the importance of self-control in life.

INDIVIDUALIZATION

Some kids need more emphasis on self-control than others. Some will enter your program with a self-control problem and will leave with the same problem but, if you have worked on it, perhaps the problem will be less severe. Others, due to insecurity or introversion, will do all right at Level I but will have problems at other levels. Still others will be model citizens. And so on.

Most of the interaction strategies can be individualized. The negotiation/confrontation process, counseling days, and praise certainly qualify in this regard, because each can be used with selected students in selected situations. The talking bench, if implemented, will only be used by those who need it, and both the first rule and teaching the levels could be used with individual students rather than be taught to the whole group. On the other hand, a formal reward system and self-officiating are group-oriented strategies.

If applied indiscriminately, self-control strategies can have negative effects. For example, too much emphasis on the first rule or on teaching the levels could bore students who are already motivated. Rewards for students who are already under control could encourage them to expect rewards for everything. Student sharing to deal with a specific student's lack of control could exacerbate the student problem. One student's criticism of my teaching was "All the big talks before class. . .After awhile it seems like he's preaching to us" (Hellison, 1978, p. 59). Perhaps a little less talk would have led to more positive interaction.

CONCLUSION

Without self-control or control imposed by some authority (you!), it is difficult if not impossible to get students involved in our subject matter. A wide range of interaction strategies and implementation ideas and cautions have been offered in this chapter. Which self-control strategies, if any, you should implement in your program will depend on your students, your setting, and your teaching style. You will need to analyze these factors, find the courage and energy to make the necessary changes, and finally evaluate the results, adjust, and try again. Once self-control has been addressed, Level II—involvement—can become the focus of attention in program planning.

CHAPTER 4

INVOLVEMENT STRATEGIES (LEVEL II)

If physical activity is perceived by the participant to be enjoyable or otherwise personally meaningful, it is more likely to become part of a daily routine upon which the participant can depend and which offers time out from daily problems and struggles. In this way, physical activity can contribute to an individual's personal stability. The current popularity of sport-fitness participation has encouraged some enthusiasts to become "over-involved" to the point that they fail to meet other obligations. Morgan (1979) has suggested that some of these individuals are negatively addicted to exercise. Levels III and IV are intended to deal with these problems.

DEVELOPMENT LEVEL II

Involvement simply refers to supervised participation in sport and exercise activities such as jumping rope, playing volleyball or crows and cranes, jogging, doing a basketball drill, trying aerobic dancing, and so on. Most physical educators, recreation leaders, and coaches see involvement as their primary goal. Whether other goals are planned or not, involvement in physical activities is clearly a priority in sport and physical education programs once students are under control.

Getting students involved in a supervised activity can be a problem, especially if the activity is new, difficult, or boring. A host of motivation factors are involved, but perceived success is perhaps the most important. In my work, I have observed a progression from play to challenge activities, and then to training and practice. Play is the easiest kind of involvement for most students. They will play basketball or four square or jump on the trampoline more readily than they will do a drill or run laps, especially if they feel they are being successful. Challenge activities which ask students "Can you do this?" and therefore require them to extend themselves are quite attractive to many kids who have past successes at challenge activities, although others would rather just play or sit around. Challenges come in many forms such as a pegboard, a rope hanging from the ceiling, a chinup bar, a handstand or headstand challenge, best out of 10 free throws, or softball throw for distance. Training refers to conditioning activities such as stretching, resistance exercises, and aerobic and anaerobic workouts. Practice refers to drills designed to improve motor skills. Both of these kinds of involvement lead to improvement but represent work to most students; therefore the motivation to do them is usually more difficult to sustain for any length of time. Of course, this play-challenge-work progression over-simplifies the very complex phenomenon of motivation, but it does serve as a useful framework for getting students involved.

INTERACTION STRATEGIES

TEACHER TALK

TEACHER-STUDENT RELATIONSHIPS

Involvement may well depend on the teacher's relationship with the student. The key is to establish a private, positive relationship so that the student feels that he/she "counts," that someone significant "cares about me." Touching bases with students individually and regularly, if even for a few seconds, really matters; the quality rather than the quantity of the interaction is what counts (Glasser, 1965). Counseling days may be very helpful here.

P.E. CAN BE "SCARY"

Monica Anderson talks to her alternative-school teenagers about
the fear often associated with trying new activities, the possibility
of failing, and so on. She says that P.E. is often scary to them.
so talking about it and showing that she is aware of their fears
can help.

THE CONCEPT OF PRACTICE

Teacher talk can be used to explain the concept of practice,
perhaps in connection with a discussion of an athlete's practice
schedule. Dolly Lambdin has done the best job I've seen of try-

ing to get her elementary school kids to understand what it takes to get better. Her journal (Lambdin, 1976) provides considerable insight into this difficulty. I remember when one of my high school students went to practice her backhand and came back 5 minutes later. "Couldn't you get court space?" I asked. "I'm finished," she replied. "I hit four backhands against the wall!"

A variation of teacher talk is to post or hand out statements stressing the importance of practice. Jerry Guthrie's workbook for youth sport, *Be Your Own Coach* (1982), talks to kids about the importance of practice as shown in the following reprint.

Practicing for the Best Learning

John Wooden, the famous UCLA basketball coach, says that a *good coach is a good teacher*. This means that a good coach knows about learning. When you are being your own coach you must decide for yourself what kinds of practice will help you learn quickly and well. Three important rules of learning can help you. They are:

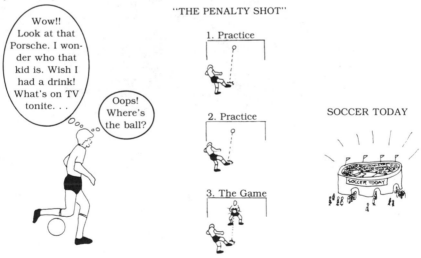

1. What you *think* when practicing is important.

2. What you practice is *exactly* what you learn.

3. You can learn by *watching* others.

*Remember, not all practice is equally effective in learning. If you use these rules of learning in the way we suggest, it will help you learn soccer skills more quickly and with less work.

Workbook Exercise

Put an X next to the statements below that are *true*:

1. ____ John Wooden says that practice is not necessary.

2. ____ Good coaches are good teachers.

3. ____ Coaches don't care about learning because players are stupid.

4. ____ This part of the workbook is about basketball.

5. ____ Good learning is influenced by what you think.

6. ____ All practice is as good as any other practice.

*Taken from *Be Your Own Coach* by Jerry Guthrie (1982). Portland: ASIEP.

MODELING

MODELING INVOLVEMENT

With smaller groups, the teacher can play with the students in order to model and reinforce involvement and proper skills; just this involvement alone may encourage students to participate. While playing, the teacher has the opportunity to model proper skills and strategies (as well as self-control behaviors) and to reinforce those students who *try* to copy, to reinforce their efforts to get better, and to point out one's own mistakes.

ATHLETES AS MODELS

If students have favorite athletes, use them as examples of hard work in order to excel. The more specific the example (e.g., time spent, number of backhands practiced each day) the better. Teachers may even be able to use themselves as examples if they can do it without sounding arrogant. Many kids I've worked with have dreams of becoming great but don't seem to connect achievement with long hours of training and practice. Of course, too much of this could be discouraging. One time I showed a film of Olympic volleyball players to my alternative-school team. It really discouraged them! They thought they were getting very good until they saw what quality really was. I tried to talk with them about the hours of practice and dedication of those players, but they weren't very responsive. On the other hand, we sometimes encourage students to dream the impossible dream rather than encourage them to acquire practical skills while they are in school.

REINFORCEMENT

GRANDMA'S LAW

A reinforcement strategy that uses play is sometimes called Grandma's Law ("Eat your soup and you can go out and play"). It is a simple "play for work" tradeoff. For example, Gayle Mac-Donald has used Grandma's Law effectively with Southeast Asian students by giving them the second half of the period to play their favorite activity (soccer or volleyball) as long as they do her activities for the first half. I've used Grandma's Law with inner-city kids to get them to experience yoga and relaxation.

A REWARD SYSTEM

In addition to its use in Grandma's Law, I've found play to be a powerful reinforcer in the more formal reward system described in Chapters 2 and 3. I tell students that they must at least "shuffle through" (thanks to Art Seavey) the activities I have lined up for several days in a row in order to earn a play day. If that works, I slowly add requirements to the play day so that they begin to experience challenges, training, and practice in activities of their choice on their earned play days (Hellison, 1978).

A letter from Steve Robbins describes his implementation of this kind of reinforcement system with 28 seventh-grade repeaters in Washington DC's inner city:

> They didn't give a damn about A's or F's. They never changed for class (with the possible exception of three of four during basketball). I tried all of the conventional methods to get them to change for class—I tried to reason with gentle talk; I tried to reason with threats of physical damage to their growing bodies; I called parents; I called administrators—nothing worked.

We were just over half-way through the school year and
90% of my class was failing for the year (or was it I that was
failing?). I had to restructure my philosophy and reprioritize
my goals and objectives. I sat down with my class and laid
out my ultimate battle plan. Since they came to me 3 days
a week, we would have required program on the first 2 days
of the week and a reward day on the third day. In the required
program, they could contract for a selected required program
of their choice. They could choose from jogging, physical
fitness, seasonal teamsport, weight training or a written program for those who did not want to participate in physical
exercise. All of the programs were sequential in difficulty, and
if a day was missed, the program could be picked up again
on an individualized basis.

I choked down my professional pride and said that no gym
clothes or showers were required to participate in the selected
program. Now we had to discuss the most important compo-
nent of the battle plan: the reward day. I innocently asked
for suggestions for possible solutions to our problem: what
would the rewards be? I was instantly bombarded with solutions: basketball (quite naturally) was the first choice by ac-
clamation. This was followed by card playing, taking up the
next step in their required programs (one small victory for
me!), and reading some magazines that I had liberated from
the library. The list grew: trampoline and badminton were
added. One student requested if he could come in and do
nothing at all; I agreed. That particular reward was listed as
"total involvement in leisure-time activity"!

To make a long story short, it worked. About 15 guys that
never changed clothes now did because they didn't want to
get their clothes dirty and now that they were engaged in
physical activities at least twice a week, they began to take
a shower as a measure of self-defense or maybe as a result
of peer group pressure. Twenty-two of the 28 passed physical
education while I still have no idea of the whereabouts of the
other six.

PRAISE

Informally reinforcing those students who show persistence at
a task increases the likelihood of continuation, especially by being honest and specific (identify what is good about what they
are doing). Persistence leads to improvement, and improvement
is a great reinforcer. Pre-post measurements of jumping, throwing, weight-lifting, and so on can help to underscore the improve-

ment. There's no better reinforcement than the activity itself, although many students have trouble sticking with an activity long enough and under appropriate learning conditions for the activity to act as a reinforcer. Fitness activities usually work better than motor skill activities because improvement is faster and more visible.

AWARDS

Giving awards in various units or activities for persistence (the "hanging in there" award) on a regular, even daily, basis will give students something besides achievement toward which to work.

SPECIFIC STRATEGIES

GIVING STUDENTS AN OUT

I've learned the hard way always to give students an "out," to loosen up the program so that they aren't backed into a corner. Forcing kids to do things they don't want to do or are afraid to do not only risks a further reduction in their motivation but sets up game-playing ("I won't do it"/"Yes you will") as well. Some strategies specific to Level II can help.

I've had the most success by giving students the option of sitting out as long as they don't bother anyone else. They don't earn credit (if applicable), but it reduces the hassle of trying to force them to participate, and it removes the usual excuses and arguments that ensue. Sitting out isn't much fun, especially if the class is enjoying the activity. If students are off task, I invite them to sit out with a loss of credit for the day. A student teacher tried his version of this by telling a student who was off task that she just lost credit for the day. As a result, he really had a problem on his hands because now the kid had nothing to lose! The key is to *offer* the option rather than mandate it.

Another approach is to offer some additional options such as jogging around the gym (or field), helping with class organization, doing a library report, or reading from some books or articles related to the unit. I've had the most success with reading assignments. Students who don't feel up to participating can read something out of a box of books I keep around, and I ask them a couple of questions about what they read at the end of the period. I give credit for this work as long as this option is only selected occasionally. Permitting a day off from time to time, especially for borderline behavior problem students, may help to keep them involved in the long run. Linda Lachey-Helms reported an upswing in participation when she introduced library reports as the only alternative to active involvement in her high school classes!

Often a teacher talk line of "try it my way for a week" may head off a student's reluctance to get involved. If after a week the student still doesn't want to be involved, a separate program may be necessary for him or her, such as a fitness program that can be observed. My experience has been that if the activity is structured to be fun, most students forget about the week and just stay involved. This is especially true for students who have had negative past experiences in the activity.

Fewer rules encourage participation. For example, a loose dress code may allow someone embarrassed by "bird legs" to wear long pants. Every rule infringes on some aspect of student freedom and is therefore a potential hindrance to involvement. Of course, student freedom does need to be restricted in some ways, but it is important to review one's rules to be certain that they are necessary and that they help more than they hinder. See Gayle MacDonald's list in Chapter 3.

If tournaments are used in physical education classes, making them optional will provide an out for those who perceive such visible winning and losing as a threat rather than as a challenge. I've done this for years at all levels of instruction, including college. Some students would rather practice than compete in a tournament!

Sometimes placing students in undemanding roles takes the pressure off them, giving them an out that still involves them to some extent in the activity (Pangrazi, 1982). For example, the goalie is most likely to be embarrassed since he/she is in a vulnerable position being the last line of defense. On the other hand, playing a wing in soccer and similar games provides action without the pressure. Less demanding and more demanding roles in all sports can be identified and used to guide students.

Being prepared to make a lesson shift when things aren't going well can keep kids interested and perhaps even attract some of those who have chosen to sit out. Good teachers can switch the order of events, invent a drill on the spot, or even change the activity without anyone knowing that the lesson plan has been changed. One teacher observed her students experimenting with headstands and handstands before class, so she set aside her tumbling lesson plan and taught headstands and handstands. Lots of times a drill or teaching method isn't working, so I just go on to the next agenda item or shift to another drill or method that seems to fit better. The lesson shift is a skill that involves sizing up students and having a repertoire of drills, methods, and the like in one's bag of tricks. Planning helps: if this happens, then I'll try X and if that happens, I'll try Y. Orlick calls this developing a solutions bank (Orlick, 1980, pp. 196-197).

CHOICES

Giving students some choices within the instructional unit or practice schedule not only gives them an "out" of sorts, but helps them to feel a bit of ownership in the program as well. As Locke and Higgins (1976) have pointed out, such ownership is minimal for kids who are denied the choices of whether to go to school or to take gym, but for those who aren't totally closed to the physical education experience, it does provide some additional involvement. It also provides a lead-up to Level III.

One of my most successful involvement strategies has been to give students the choice of intensity (or meaning) in playing a particular activity. If the facility can be organized to offer three stations of basketball, volleyball, soccer, or whatever (that is, three baskets, three nets, or three goals), three choices can be offered: blood and guts (competitive), hit and giggle (recreational), or practice. Students who want to be less competitive have that option, and students who would rather just work on shooting (with the help of task card progressions or challenges) can do that. Pam McCammon reports that her sixth graders' eyes sparkled when she introduced these choices. Gary Kuney, an elementary teacher, gives his students in a track unit the choice of run-and-compete or jog-and-giggle!

Gary Pennington gives students a 5 × 8 card that lists 15 to 20 challenges from which they must try a certain number. Students record their scores on the card which provides space for three trials. They have some choice in this approach, yet they are encouraged to extend themselves in whatever they choose. Challenges could include best of 10 free throws, timed juggling, throwing accuracy, number of pushups, and so on.

Just asking students what they want to do may help them feel involved if the teacher follows up on some of their suggestions. I've had some success in turning 1 day a week over to the kids to plan.

Movement exploration (e.g., see Turner & Turner, 1976) gives kids a sense of ownership by encouraging them to find their own ways of solving movement problems. I've even done some of this with high school kids. Other individualized instruction strategies discussed in the next chapter may have a similar effect.

PLAY AS MOTIVATION

Sometimes play can be used to get students involved. Here are several strategies that rely on play to help students learn and improve skills.

One such approach is to substitute play-teach-play for demonstration-drill-play so that students can try the activity or some modification (such as six-aside soccer) before they are given any instruction other than a couple of rules. Play can be stopped after a few minutes to give them one or two tips, then they can go back and play some more. For example, in soccer I usually give them some simple strategies first (don't bunch, triangle formations, movement off the ball), let them play some more, then introduce skills. This approach is usually palatable to most kids, and they are more likely to see the need for instruction after struggling to master the activity in its game form. This technique can work in organized sport as well, especially if the students find it difficult to pay attention to formal instruction. Safety needs to be considered when implementing this strategy (thanks to Linda Lachey-Helms). For example, playing at archery without some firm guidelines could be disastrous. The same goes for trampoline and several other activities.

Another play-oriented approach is to move from the familiar to the unfamiliar. Basketball is a popular activity with many city kids. Trampoline is always popular (if allowed where you teach). Volleyball is easy (especially if students employ the "tree theory" which involves standing around like trees), and the net reduces team sport problems by separating the teams. Research suggests that alienated youth are less likely to be attracted to competitive team sports (Yiannakis, 1980), but I've only experienced a little of this. The idea here is to work from the familiar to the unfamiliar, recognizing where students "are at" before introducing new skills and concepts.

Sometimes play in a physical education class can evolve into formal instruction if students become motivated. Once students are playing the teacher may be able to get away with some formal instruction. At first this might be the result of teachable moments during which a particular skill or strategy worked for some student; later it could be a more planned progression. I've had some success in an alternative-school class of 15 students, moving them from "tree theory/jungle rules" volleyball to skill instruction with drills (of all things) and eventually to competition against another school during class time. Organizing some kind of competition with another class or school (or intraclass) provides an opportunity to train and practice toward a specific goal, much the same as interscholastic athletic competition. The skills may not be the same, but the intent and motivation are quite similar.

CHALLENGES

The concept of a challenge can be used to get students more involved. Pennington's challenge choices is one idea. Here are five others.

Challenge activities can consist of bettering one's initial score or achieving one's personal best, thus building individualization into the process. For example, the survival bar hang (above an imaginary snake pit?) challenges students to hang as long as they can and in subsequent tries to better their first score. The use of a wide variety of pre- and posttests, preferably over a few months, can give students who show improvement considerable reinforcement for their involvement, especially if improvement and personal bests are emphasized rather than winners and norms. Just having challenging things for kids to do is an informal approach which some teachers have found to be effective.

Some kids respond to personal challenges. I remember a volleyball unit in a Los Angeles inner-city high school. One student thought it was "stupid," so I challenged him and some of his pals to a volleyball game. I enlisted for my team a group of kids who were standing around, and jabbed at the scoffers throughout the match. They got mad and really put out a big effort to beat us. This can backfire, of course; the key is to bait students into involvement without carrying it too far.

Morris and Stiehl (in press) argue for game modifications that will both include everybody and challenge everybody. For example, they modified a kickball game so that everyone on the fielding team had to touch the ball after it was kicked. To challenge everyone, each player had to stand inside a hoop on the field when touching the ball. By placing each player's hoop closer to other players or farther away, catching and throwing could be made more or less challenging.

Some activities provide built-in challenge in the participation itself. Ropes courses, trust falls, and the like (Rohnke, 1977; Darst & Armstrong, 1980) fall in this category, especially if the student can choose the degree of difficulty. Combative activities also offer built-in anxiety; it doesn't matter whether you win or lose, or execute the skill properly, but whether you can avoid being hit! Safety is obviously a concern, but I've had considerable success getting kids involved in combative activities without injuries. Strategies include: emphasizing skills, footwork, and fitness; using lots of shadow sparring and heavy bag or mat or football dummy punching and kicking; allowing students only to spar with me; placing a line between students which neither can cross; sparring with nondominant hand only.

Bill White requires all of his students to perform in front of other students at the end of the gymnastics unit, thereby building a particular kind of challenge into his program. He is a talented

teacher who can pull this off by mixing encouragement with humor. My impression is that his students not only practice to get ready but really enjoy the experience. Kathlyn Williams requires her coed class to divide into groups of two and to create routines to be performed at the end of the unit. At performance time she allows them to choose whether both will perform or one will perform while the other gives directions. Pangrazi (1982) has suggested requiring students to practice but giving them a choice of when to perform.

ORGANIZED SPORT

Some involvement problems are specific to organized sport. Two such problems are described in the following paragraphs.

Much has been written about the overemphasis on winning in organized sport. Pam Yoder plays with her high school varsity basketball team "just for fun" on a regular basis to remind her players that it is just a game and that having fun is important. Several years ago a former student of mine, Kit Cody (1976), tried to change Portland's city-wide youth wrestling program so that winners and losers of matches were neither announced nor were cumulative statistics kept. He didn't want to change the game, just the trappings. For example, a pin would still end the match, but no one's hand would be held up in victory and no one's win-loss record would be recorded. Kit succeeded in convincing the coaches to keep no team scores, but could not get their full cooperation. Martens' *Joy and Sadness in Children's Sport* (1978) argues repeatedly and articulately for youth sport programs that place fun and a striving for excellence, health, and self-confidence above winning.

Recently, considerable attention has been paid to the problem of getting the most out of one's physical potential in sport—that is, becoming fully involved. I like Orlick's (1980) approach to this problem. He advocates helping athletes determine their level of commitment, followed by the selection and implementation of those strategies that appear most able to deliver on this commitment. He presents a number of strategies such as goal setting, mental imagery, simulation, "inner sport," and the rational approach, but emphasizes that each athlete must select those that work for him or her. The coach's role is one of adviser/helper rather than director/group leader in this individualized process.

CURRICULUM CONSIDERATIONS

You don't need to implement any involvement strategies if all your students are fully involved in your program activities. However, even the best programs include some range of motivation among students. One way to determine whether you want to make any changes is to ask whether any of the involvement strategies would improve your program. For example:

1. One group of strategies—giving students an out—is designed to loosen up the program. It gives kids who don't like what's going on, or who are afraid (either physically or psychologically), some room to become involved in their own way. Would any of these strategies help any of your students? Put another way, do you have any students who are reluctant to participate or who downright refuse? You might talk with them and find out their reasons. We often give our own reasons for the lack of motivation, reasons which come from our own experiences rather than theirs. However, if such strategies would reduce involvement by giving kids excuses for not participating or by teaching them that everything is negotiable,

then they obviously shouldn't be used. The intention is to increase involvement, not to reduce it.

2. Another group of strategies—choices—also serves to loosen up the program and, in addition, to give kids some sense of ownership in the program. I remember how surprised I was to see the reaction of sixth-graders to choosing a blood and guts track meet, a hit and giggle track meet, or jogging and taking pulse rates. About a third of the kids went to each station, and afterward they shared ideas on how to improve or change the options. Would a sense of ownership help your students feel more involved?

3. Still another group of strategies—play as motivation—uses play to introduce or encourage learning. Are your kids play-oriented? Do they have difficulty staying on task for skill drills or fitness routines? Do they need to be led into greater involvement?

4. Other involvement strategies—reinforcement, modeling, and teacher talk, as well as the concept of challenge—might also be useful in helping students become more involved and more successful. Do any of your students need to be told or shown that they are getting better or making a good effort? Would a stronger relationship with you help any of them? Would awareness of the training schedules of famous athletes help? Do they understand the concept of practice? Do they need to be challenged in some way?

5. Strategies specific to organized sport respond to these questions: Does winning need to be downplayed to increase involvement? Do your athletes need help in concentrating or help with other problems that reduce the actualization of their physical potentialities?

Some of these strategies can be integrated into your program without changing the focus at all, for example, the "giving students an out" strategies and individual reinforcement. Others change the focus slightly, such as play-teach-play, and choice of blood and guts or hit and giggle. Strategies such as a reinforcement system or a ropes course will require more substantial changes. Times can be set aside specifically to work on greater involvement if it is a problem, or time can be used simply to focus on exposure, play, and improvement in a variety of activities. For example, Gayle MacDonald, Tom Hinton, and Pam Yoder designate two periods a week (out of five) as activity days in which the primary goal is involvement in new activities and in learning.

INDIVIDUALIZATION

Depending on past successes and failures as well as other factors, some students need more encouragement at Level II than others. Some don't even care to play. Others will play and that's it. Still others will be motivated by challenges to improve. Some will enthusiastically train and practice, whereas others will be interested in only specific activities or tasks.

Many of the involvement strategies can be individualized. Individual feedback, individual teacher-student relationships, personal challenges, and explaining the concept of practice are examples of strategies that can be implemented with individual students as needed. All of the loosening-up strategies can be individually applied; you can pull them from your bag of tricks to use as you see fit. One student may need an out, whereas another may need to be confronted (Chapter 3). The skill, of course, lies in making the right application each time. The ownership strategies are designed for the entire group, but since these strategies give everyone some choice or voice in what goes on, they enhance the individualization process. So does Orlick's approach for becoming fully involved in organized sport.

Your individual teaching style will dictate to what extent any of these strategies will be useful to you. Playing with your students, play-teach-play, giving challenge choices—these and other strategies may or may not fit your teaching style.

CONCLUSION

Involvement is the major goal of most teachers. This entails introducing students to new subject matter and helping them to improve in activities with which they are already familiar. Lack of control—that is, discipline problems—often gets in the way of involvement. That's why self-control is first in the developmental levels. However, inadequate involvement strategies often cause a problem. This chapter has described a wide range of involvement strategies and implementation ideas. Again, it's up to you to size up your situation and follow through by making the appropriate changes. Once involvement is under way, Level III—self-responsibility—can become the focus of attention.

CHAPTER 5

SELF-RESPONSIBILITY STRATEGIES (LEVEL III)

We live in a time of rapid social change, economic uncertainty, and changing ethical values. More choices are open to all of us, choices involving direction and purpose, and there are fewer firm guidelines to help us make personal and social decisions or even to deter us from making choices that will be harmful to ourselves and/or others. The results of these trends have been mixed. Insecurity, anxiety, and isolation have increased as people search for themselves and try to "do their own thing," bouncing from one activity to another, from one relationship to another, from one identity to another. At the same time, quality-of-life issues are being raised more than ever, and some individuals have flourished in the new freedom to become unique, personally productive, and happy. Also, marginal lifestyles have become more acceptable, thereby allowing some to come out of hiding or to search more openly for suitable options.

For today's youth, two needs emerge from these trends. First, more than ever before, kids need to learn to make responsible choices. As Johnson (1980, p. 11) points out, the need for personal decision-making skills is not new:

> Everyone needs. . .processes such as directing one's attention toward desired future goals. . .believing that one is in control of one's fate and can take initiative in applying one's

resources toward the achievement of one's goals, feeling satisfaction when a meaningful goal is achieved, and utilizing one's potentialities to achieve one's goals.

It's just that these processes are more crucial in today's world. Second, kids need to develop a positive sense of who they are, a "strong and integrated personal identity. . .which will serve as an anchor in life" (Johnson, 1980, p. 12). These two needs are linked. A personal choice may be responsible in that it serves its intended purpose, for example, by creating a feeling of satisfaction or by utilizing one's potentialities; but continually lurching from choice to choice with reckless abandon may well lead to an identity crisis rather than to an integrated sense of self. Our society has supported the notion of individual freedom and responsibility since the Declaration of Independence. Current trends are creating needs that force us to take another look at this value, particularly how we are going to make it work.

DEVELOPMENTAL LEVEL III

Level II, involvement, refers to participation in sport and exercise, usually under adult supervision. By contrast, Level III, self-responsibility, means working and playing independently—that is, without the need for direct supervision. Students at Level III are able to work on their own without being prompted and prodded to stay on task. Moreover, they can make and deliver on personal preference choices which are in line with Level I's self-control imperative and also contribute to their own sense of identity. The following guidelines more fully describe the attitudes and behaviors of Level III.

LEVEL III GUIDELINES

ACCEPTING RESPONSIBILITY

Students should assume a reasonable responsibility for their attitudes and actions. All of us have some degree of freedom to make choices, and yet we are limited by our genetic inheritance, our past learning experiences, and circumstances beyond our control. This simply means that students can be encouraged to assume more responsibility for what they think, say, and do. It can be as simple as cutting down on excuses and on blaming others by substituting "It's my problem" or "I just blew it, that's all," or "She was better than I was today." It can be as simple as saying "thank you" when they are complimented. It can be as simple as doing a drill without supervision. It can also be as complicated as separating fantasies that make them feel good from goals that they want to achieve.

DELIVERING ON PROMISES

A related guideline to becoming self-responsible is for students to deliver on their promises, to match their words with actions. Talk flows easily; backing up these words with deeds is more difficult. Examples in sport and exercise abound. It is not uncommon to hear someone tell of a personal exercise plan that somehow never gets implemented, and kids are forever announcing their intentions to achieve or participate in a particular sport without following through. Being responsible in this sense does not necessarily require more action; it *does* require an adjustment in either words or behavior so that they more closely match each other. Of course, fantasies can be fun, but they should be recognized as fantasies. Then again, unreachable goals and fantasies are often used to cover up perceived inadequacies and, as a result, may provide some short-term protection for the individual. In the long run, however, helping students to close the gap between their verbal goals, plans, and promises and their behavior will contribute both to making responsible choices and to a more integrated identity in the sense of achieving a better fit between words and actions.

GOAL SETTING

Students must learn to set some attainable goals for themselves. Goals imply the identification of personal preferences that require work in order to be realized. As Gayle MacDonald has observed of her inner-city high school students, "I've never met a student who didn't want to improve his or her body in some way." Goals can be short-term such as setting aside some time on a regular basis to improve free throwing or long-term such as a weight control program. They can be few or numerous. Sport and physical education goals can be related to achievement, self-improvement, health maintenance, play-attitude development, and/or adventure seeking. Goals can build on strengths, can strengthen weaknesses, or both.

Much has been made of poor self-concept and low self-esteem as barriers to student development. Indeed, some students work very hard to protect their inadequacies or embrace their identity as problem kids (anti-heroes). Reinforcement of good behavior sometimes only encourages these students to work harder at being inadequate or bad, and self-reflection can be overwhelming if everything one does and stands for appears to need work. These students may respond to setting a goal in relation to a strength they know they already possess, for example jumping rope or swimming or basketball. Others respond to setting a goal that represents a value or an identity need such as weight training, weight control, or whatever game is currently popular at recess. The point is to find something the student is willing to work toward, that is meaningful to him or her, and then to build on this process.

All of us need health, self-development, adventure, and play in our lives; however, the percentages and specific activities vary considerably from person to person. Some of us are more sensitive to peer pressure and the social comparison process and need to prove ourselves in relation to cultural, group, or sex role standards. Lyon (1971) calls this *self-image actualizing* and argues that, for many of us, self-image actualizing must take place before true self-actualizing of our interests and potentials can begin. Students can be educated about this process and their place in it. They can identify things that they would like to do and be, and things that they need to do and be in order to be okay with themselves and, if necessary, others. They can analyze the pressures on them to do this or that, and determine to what extent these pressures are appropriate motivating forces in their worlds. They can check their goals against existing standards and compare them to the most popular play forms. Can these activities help them to develop or should they look for other avenues? They can assess their own energy levels to determine what it will take to achieve their goals.

DEVELOPING A KNOWLEDGE BASE

A knowledge base is necessary in order to carry out personal goals. If a student desires to lose weight, doing situps or using a health spa shake machine won't help much; the concept of caloric expenditure must be understood. If a student desires to learn a new skill or refine an old one, then the learning process must be understood. The student needs at least to have a mental picture of the skill, to practice, and to get feedback.

GOAL IMPLEMENTATION

Goals must be implemented and evaluated to be effective. For example, de Charms (1976) improved both short- and long-term student motivation and student achievement among inner-city fifth to eighth graders by teaching students:

1. to prepare their plan carefully;

2. to practice the skills in their plan;

3. to persist in their plan;

4. to have patience;

5. to check their progress and pay attention to their improvement.

His research (1976, 1979) points out the importance of implementing and evaluating personal goals. To accomplish this, de Charms focused on "increasing the pupils' experience of their own control in the classroom, up to a point, and decreasing the teacher's attempts to maintain strict control" (de Charms, 1979, p. 35).

GOALS AS PROCESS

Excellence by definition is reserved for a few in every endeavor, but self-change is a never-ending process that can be experienced by all. Short-term goals are reinforcing, and lots of goals may lead to success somewhere. But whether goals are short-term or long-term, few or many, achievement-oriented or improvement-oriented, they are all part of a life process. Winning the Super Bowl doesn't mean that the process stops and participants can spend the rest of their lives reliving that achievement. It's not that achievements and personal bests along the way don't count; the point is that everything is a part of a lifetime process. That process, as it is carried out, reflects significant themes in our lives and therefore gives each of us a personal identity. As a Nike poster says, "There is no finish line."

THE ROLE OF SPONTANEITY

It is important to recognize that spontaneity plays an important role in life. We don't want to encourage students to plan every move they make, thereby sacrificing all spontaneity other than flukes of luck and circumstance. As in so many things, balance is necessary—in this case a balance between planning and spontaneity. Level III involves deciding how much planning and how much spontaneity one needs in his/her life to achieve happiness, a sense of personal productivity, and a positive identity. This is an individual decision, but the guideline suggests that some planning and some spontaneity will be useful. How much planning and, interestingly, how much spontaneity is built into the plan depends on the individual. For one person, intending to do something sometime in the next month may be enough; mapping out the day-to-day details of a specific plan is not necessary. For some, planning a celebration time actually helps it to happen; others celebrate freely without planning. For one person, knowing that he can "pay his rent" the next day permits him to indulge himself (Shepro & Knuttgen, 1979, pp. 112-115); others need to plan better to reduce the indulging. Some need to overload while others need to avoid "over-overloading" and so on. The measure of success here is simply what works for the student. If actions or impulses seem to work, the planning process can be introduced as a back-up, supplemental system.

SENSE OF HUMOR

The last guideline is a reminder not to take oneself too seriously. Keep some spontaneity and also keep a sense of humor. Students can be encouraged to put self-change in perspective by being able to laugh at their own stumbling and fumbling as they try to become more responsible for their thoughts and actions.

INTERACTION STRATEGIES

TEACHER TALK

INCREASING STUDENT RESPONSIBILITY

Most students aren't used to making and carrying out choices that are personally productive and that lead to a stable, integrated sense of self (or identity). They need to be prepared to do so. Teacher talk can help set the stage. "It's your body and your life!" I can't count how many times I've said that to my students in response to their efforts to make their problems my problems. "Your behavior is all you can control" or "I'll pull (help), but you have to push" are other one-liners that keep the concept of self-responsibility in front of students. "To get better you have to pay the price" is yet another. I also tell students that they need to bear down on themselves, to create their own structures and then live by them rather than waiting for me to create the structure or acting as if they need no structure. All of these have somewhat belligerent, you'd-better-listen undertones and no doubt represent some of my frustrations. The same idea can be conveyed gently and supportively as in "Didn't you say you were going to. . .?"

Even at the university level, I continually remind my students that they have choices, that it is their body, that they are responsible for their own goals and plans. Teachers can also talk to their students about self-change as a process versus trying to be objectively excellent. They can encourage students to identify their strengths, to assess their needs, to become aware of peer pressure and other influences, to laugh at themselves, to accept what they can't change, and to be better. They can share their own needs, their own struggles, their own foolishness. I've held individual talks and group talks along these lines. Individual talks can include dialog: "What do you think?" and should be tailored to the individual. Group talks which remind students of their responsibility are usually followed by a flurry of independent activity (which soon dies out!).

TEACHING CONCEPTS

Teacher talk coupled with activities designed to teach concepts can help students understand that they are capable of improving their body on their own. For example, if they understand the principles of overload and specificity (without necessarily using those terms), they will be better equipped to develop an exercise program. If they understand practice and feedback, they will be better equipped to learn or improve a skill on their own. Many sources are available for this purpose (Corbin & Lindsey, 1983; the Basic Stuff Series, 1981). There are several ways to teach concepts. We have had some success at both the elementary and secondary level by teaching concepts while doing an activity and also as part of the explanation of what students are to do. Other methods are posting the concepts, testing students orally and sometimes in writing on their comprehension, and requiring some comprehension for independent work (e.g., as prerequisite to making a contract). Bill White teaches concepts to his high school gymnasts and wrestlers; for example, he explains the overload principle so that students understand the necessity of weight training and can weight train independently. He also teaches nutrition principles so that wrestlers can control their weight sensibly and on their own. Gayle MacDonald hands out a photocopy of some Peanuts cartoons with these captions:

In this class we are all students and we are all teachers.

1. Mental image: Imagine in your mind's eye what it looks like when done right.

2. Repetition: Practice the skill many times even though you don't do it right and may look very silly.

3. Feedback: Ask someone to watch you and tell you what you're doing right and wrong.

She also conducts laboratories for her students to help them understand concepts. Here is one of her labs:

Lab Exercise

Name _____

STATEMENT: Different activities will cause your heart rate to beat at different
speeds.

Exercise:

1. After you shoot baskets for two minutes what is your HR (heart rate) per
   minute?

2. After you do push-ups for two minutes what is your HR/minute?

3. After you sit for two minutes what is your HR/minute?

4. After you jump rope for two minutes what is your HR/minute?

5. After you do curl-ups for two minutes what is your HR/minute?

6. After you tumble for two minutes what is your HR/minute?

7. After you jog for two minutes what is your HR/minute?

Conclusions:

1. Which two activities from this lab seem to give the heart the most exercise?

2. Which two activities from this lab seem to give the heart the least exercise?

3. What are two other activities that might give the heart a great deal of
   exercise?

Fitness and skill concepts help set the stage for Level III; they are also useful after students have made individual plans which require that they understand the concepts in order to carry out the plans.

MODELING (BEING)

Modeling can also help set the stage. Every time teachers are able to show self-responsibility by their own example they are modeling self-responsibility. Every time they deliver on a promise such as "tomorrow I'll have a tournament set up for those who want one" or "tomorrow we'll scrimmage," they demonstrate responsibility for their intentions. Every time they make a bad pass or shot or hit in a game and say "I blew that one" they demonstrate responsibility for their actions. When I fail to be responsible, as I often do, we talk about it. I share my intentions and admit my failure to carry them out.

It is also important to model spontaneity and a sense of humor while—not instead of—helping students to become more responsible. These qualities form the spice of self-responsibility, preventing the process from becoming too plodding and unimaginative.

REINFORCEMENT

PRAISE

Praise can be used to prepare students for independent work. Outside of reinforcement from the process of being responsible itself, the best approach to the reinforcement of independent activity involves praise when students accept responsibility or show independence.

CHARTING PROGRESS

Students can be taught to chart their own progress on a wall chart or in a journal. This reinforces their efforts and at the same time emphasizes their individuality and capacity for improvement. Pam Yoder has her high school basketball team record their feats and improvements. She reports that "they can't wait to write them down." In his book, *Be Your Own Coach* (1982),

Jerry Guthrie teaches young athletes how to track their own progress. The following are excerpts:

Measuring Improvement

When you practice with a coach he/she looks for improvements in your skills and fitness. Without a coach, you must make your own decisions about which skills need work or what kind of conditioning to do. To make good decisions you need to: (1) *measure* your skills and fitness and (2) make some kind of *comparison* to determine progress.

Measurements

You can measure soccer skills and body fitness in several ways:

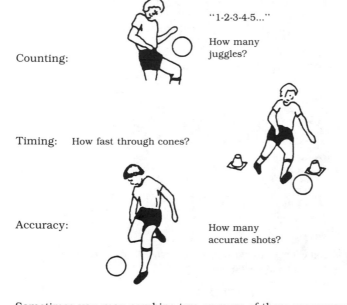

Counting:

"1-2-3-4-5..."

How many juggles?

Timing: How fast through cones?

Accuracy:

How many accurate shots?

Sometimes you may combine two or more of these measurements.

"How many hops over the ball in 30 seconds?"

Measuring Improvement (Cont.)

Comparisons

You can compare your performance measurements with other players. This tells you how you are doing *compared to others*.

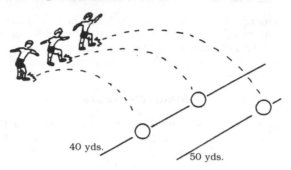

In most self-coached practice and fitness training the best comparisons are with *your own past records*.

These comparisons make it easy to see your improvement. Such *personal records* are very important in good self-coaching.

Exercise

1. How would you measure each of these skills?

   Juggling _____   Trapping _____

   Dribbling _____   Shooting _____

2. Last week you ran a mile in 11 minutes. This week you ran it in 10 minutes. What kind of comparison is this? _____

3. Most 12-year-olds can kick a soccer ball 40 yards. You are 12 and can kick it 50 yards. What kind of comparison is this? _____

Record Keeping Tips

Keeping regular and accurate records of your self-coached practice is easy when you follow a few simple ideas:

1. *Keep your recording simple and convenient.* A small 3 × 5 index card or notebook can be easily carried and makes recording your skill measurements regular. Don't trust your memory—write it down!

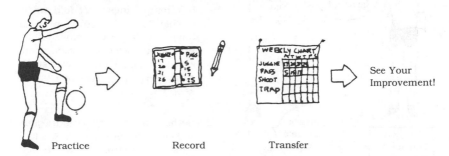

Practice   Record   Transfer   See Your
                                                                   Improvement!

2. *Transfer your measurements from the small record to a permanent chart.* A wall chart posted in a conspicuous place will allow you to see how your measurements look over a long period of time.

Remember, practicing for measurement is a useful way of spending some of your practice time. It is not a substitute for the challenge and joy that you have when you play under match conditions. Goals scored, shots taken, good dribbling runs and effective crosses are the measurements that are important to the game.

Exercise

Put an X in front of the statements below that are true:

1. ____ All records should be kept indoors.

2. ____ You should keep your wall chart in a secret place.

3. ____ It is more fun to keep records than play soccer.

Record Keeping for Self-Coaching

When you *write* your *performance* measurements you are keeping records. Self-coached practice is made more effective if you keep good records. Good records will help you:

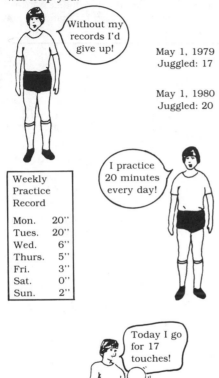

1. *See small, gradual improvements in your skill.* Can you remember how many times you could juggle the ball 8 months ago? How much have you improved since then? When you are feeling discouraged, a record that shows even small gains can pick up your spirits and keep you going.

2. *Be honest and accurate in your self-comparisons.* Often we fool ourselves into thinking we are better or worse than we really are. Written records can help you see clearly how often you have practiced and how much you have improved. They make it harder to fool yourself.

3. *Set realistic goals for yourself.* Goals are statements about what you would like to achieve in your performance. *Long-term* goals are those that are far in the future. *Short-term* goals are those that you can reach quickly. Long-term goals sometimes seem impossible to reach, but if you break these distant goals into small steps then you will not get discouraged. Records show you how each step adds up.

Exercise

When you write down your skill measurements you are keeping (1) _____.
Records help you notice (2) _____ in skill. Records help you set (3) _____ for yourself. If you keep good records it is easier to be (4) _____ with yourself about how often you practice and how much you have improved. If you get discouraged trying to reach (5) _____ - _____ goals break them down in smaller _____ - _____ goals.

Gayle MacDonald uses the following "Body Profile" to help her students see improvement. Involvement is reinforced and, if they do it themselves, self-responsibility is reinforced as well.

Body Profile

Fitness Test:	Fall	Winter	Improvement

Flexibility

1. Sit and reach

2. Arm and shoulder reach

3. Trunk lift

4. Trunk twist

5.

Cardiovascular

1. Step test

2. 1-mile jog

Muscular Endurance

1. Half sit-ups

2. Push-ups

3. Chin-ups

4. Lower body lift

5.

Others

1. Vertical jump

2. 50-yard dash

3. Agility

Body Measurements:

Bicep (arm)

Neck

Chest

Body Profile (Cont.)

Waist

Hips

Thigh

Calf

Weight

Height

Fitness Test: *Spring*   *Improvement*

Flexibility

1. Sit and reach

2. Arm and shoulder reach

3. Trunk lift

4. Trunk twist

5.

Cardiovascular

1. Step test

2. 1-mile jog

Muscular Endurance

1. Half sit-ups

2. Push-ups

3. Chin-ups

4. Lower body lift

5.

Others

1. Vertical jump

2. 50-yard dash

3. Agility

Body Profile (Cont.)

Body Measurements:

Bicep (arm)

Neck

Chest

Waist

Hips

Thigh

Calf

Weight

Height

A REWARD SYSTEM

A reward system can be used to reinforce students who have met certain requirements by giving them some independent work and play time, thereby using responsibility as both a requirement and a reward. Requirements usually include demonstrating responsible behavior, mastery of relevant concepts, and some level of experience and success in teacher-directed activities. In this approach, students earn the right to work and play independently of the teacher. Goals, a specific plan, and a method of evaluation may be required, depending on the sophistication of the students. How much time is allowed for independent work and what space is designated for it can vary greatly depending on the teacher's style, setting, and students. Emotionally handicapped youngsters ages 7 through 12 have successfully carried out this kind of independence under Kim Weaver's direction, as have inner-city "problem" teenagers in a couple of my programs (Hellison, 1978). I've also used this approach with a high school wrestling team by giving them some independence during fitness time in return for good attendance and effort during practice.

Jeff Walsh divides his days for independent work and play into teacher time and student time. Jeff visits the various stations where students who have earned clean days (i.e., met the requirements) are on student time carrying out their contracts. When he arrives, those students shift from student time to teacher time to receive some instruction from him. When he leaves they go back to student time. Students who have not earned enough clean days (four in a row in his program) stay with Jeff the whole period. That way they receive instruction and practice time in a variety of activities while remaining under his control. This of course emphasizes self-control as well as self-responsibility.

One physical education teacher in a Chicago inner-city vocational school wrote this to me:

> Your clean days method for dealing with problem kids and your method of contracts is innovative and modern. It allows the student the respect he/she should have and it also allows them freedom to choose what's good for their particular situation. When school starts in September, I am going to use your method in dealing with my classes. In reality, we have the same type of students to work with. My results should be achieved a lot faster than yours because all my students are black, and I've worked at the same school for thirteen years. I choose to use your method because my failure rate has been high for my classes the past three years. I should be innovative as you, and try something new. I feel in our society today that the conventional approach to education and the methods of teaching will have to change with the times if it's to be as successful as it was in the past.

MODIFIED REWARD SYSTEMS

A related approach is to permit everyone to try independence by designating space, alotting a specific time period, and giving guidelines (thanks to Don Bethe). Those who have trouble staying on task could be brought back under teacher control, not in the form of some punitive activity such as running laps but instead with some instruction and activity in whatever the class has been doing. The courage to make and carry out an individual plan can be reinforced just by offering some freedom from teacher control to those who demonstrate the courage to try to set personal goals.

AWARDS

Once again, awards can be given periodically to reinforce Level III activity such as independence, goal-setting, following through, and so on.

REFLECTION TIME

PAUSE AND THINK

Any post-lesson effort to encourage students to reflect on the extent of their responsible thoughts and acts during the lesson will be helpful. Examples are requiring short entries in a journal, grading their level of responsibility, checking off those activities they did that day, or asking them which word best summarizes their actions that day. A related kind of reflection asks students whether their actions, especially if they had some choice, "worked for them" and if not, whether they plan to do the same thing again.

QUESTIONNAIRES

Self-reflection can be used to help students assess their strengths, needs, and interests as a prerequisite to setting more specific goals for themselves. Journals and counseling days which have already been described can be used for this purpose; so can the following reflection time questionnaires and forms that have been specifically designed to help students develop Level III plans.

Peter Teppler uses the following "Big Ideas Sheet" to help his high school students think about their own goals.

Bob Blanchette, who works with Peter, uses student sharing to have his students create their own self-inventory by suggesting what they feel are characteristics of being responsible and irresponsible.

Big Ideas Sheet

A. Goal

Self-Responsibility

B. Definition

Setting reasonable goals that force you to extend yourself in reaching them. If you *don't* reach your goal after you have:

1. attempted to reach the goal in a reasonable length of time,

2. determined it to be an "inbounds" (achievable, attainable) goal,

You *must* figure out why you didn't completely reach your goal.

C. Reasons for Valuing the Goal

Being self-directed as opposed to being externally directed all the time will help you "go and grow" in directions you see yourself having to go rather than in directions others see you as having to go. It will help you fulfill your expectations of yourself. You will "take charge" of your fate.

D. Self-Inventory

CODE: 5 (Very Often)
         4 (Frequently)
         3 (Occasionally)
         2 (Seldom)
         1 (Never)

I Am Responsible If:			I Am Not Responsible If:	
I often think about where I'm going in life.			I never think about where I'm going.	
5	4	3	2	1
I know what I value enough to work toward.			I'm always working toward ends that others have set for me.	
5	4	3	2	1
I know myself well enough to set reasonable (inbounds) goals.			I set goals for myself on whim that I have no hope of achieving.	
5	4	3	2	1

Big Ideas Sheet (Cont.)

I have some immediate goals (ones that I can achieve soon) and some long-range goals.		All my goals are long-range goals and my commitment to them wanes over that long period of time.

     5   4   3   2   1

I'm secure enough to admit that there are things that I can't do well and others can help me to meet my goals.		I know it all and anything I can't do now isn't worth doing anyway.

     5   4   3   2   1

I have detailed plans to allow me to become the kind of person I wish to become.		I only daydream about things I would like to be or do.

     5   4   3   2   1

I don't need a lot of people (parents, teachers, etc.) pushing on me to get things done.		I need to be brided, threatened, blackmailed and intimidated into doing things.

     5   4   3   2   1

I persevere. I'll try many, many times before I'll quit or give up.		I quit or give up at the first sign of problems.

     5   4   3   2   1

I take responsibility for my failures and successes.		I blame others for goals I've failed to achieve.

     5   4   3   2   1

I look realistically at why I failed, when I do fail.		I don't give much thought to why I did not meet goals I've set for myself.

     5   4   3   2   1

I've used the following self-report to help students assess their body image and perceived performance and to determine to what extent they desire to get better.

Self-Report

Name _____

Health				Desire to Improve		

Body fat: I have

Too much	Enough	Too little		Yes	No	Don't care

Cardiovascular endurance: I can

Run 2 miles in 12 min.	Jog a mile	Get out of breath easily		Yes	No	Don't care

Flexibility: I can

Touch my toes easily	Touch my toes barely	Not reach my toes	Not reach much beyond my knees	Yes	No	Don't care

Self-Report (Cont.)

Relaxation: I can

Never seem to relax	Relax some-times	Relax whenever I want to		Yes	No	Don't care

Safety

Strength: I am

Very strong	Strong enough to take care of myself in an emergency	Too weak to take care of myself in an emer-gency		Yes	No	Don't care

Speed: I can run away from trouble

If my assail-ants have broken legs	In some situ-ations	Usually	Almost always	Yes	No	Don't care

Self-defense: My self-defense skills are good enough to

Get me in deep trouble	Help me a little bit	Help me in most situations	Help me in any situation I can imagine	Yes	No	Don't care

Water safety: I can swim, float, and tread water for

Over an hour	Over 30 min.	At least 15 min.	Glub-Glub	Yes	No	Don't care

Behavior

Desire to Improve

While I am playing or working out, I will help someone else:

Never	If it is an emergency	Usually, if someone needs help	Any time some-one needs help	Yes	No	Don't care

In situations that are physically risky or dangerous or a threat to my body's safety, I:

Avoid these situations if possible	Am scared but face these situations	Enjoy these sit-uations		Yes	No	Don't care

Self-Report (Cont.)

As far as I am concerned, playing fair is:

The most important thing in playing a sport or game	Of some importance to me.	Of little importance when I play a sport or game	Yes	No	Don't care

In sports and games, I:

Show how angry and frustrated I am.	Sometimes control my anger and frustration.	Always control my anger and frustration.	Yes	No	Don't care

When I have the opportunity to push myself beyond being physically comfortable I:

Push myself as far as I can.	Push myself a little beyond what is comfortable.	Avoid these situations if possible.	Yes	No	Don't care

Appearance

My body is

Muscular		Soft	Yes	No	Don't care
Heavy	Just right	Light	Yes	No	Don't care

My posture is:

Poor	Average	Good	Yes	No	Don't care

Gayle MacDonald has developed her own "self-report" to fit her inner-city school situation.

PERCEIVED CAUSES OF SUCCESS AND FAILURE

A slightly different approach utilizes attribution theory (Roberts, 1977) to ask students to what they attribute their skill, fit-

Self-Report (Cont.)

Name _____

Achievement and Play

I am. . .

	A pro	Varsity level	Above average	Average	Below average	Poor	Never did it	Enjoy it	Would like to improve
Badminton									
Basketball									
Bowling									
Boxing									
Canoing/ Kayaking									
Cycling									
Dance									
Fencing									
Fishing									
Fitness									
Football									
Golf									
Gymnastics									
Handball									

Self-Report (Cont.)

Achievement and Play

I am. . .

	A pro	Varsity level	Above average	Average	Below average	Poor	Never did it	Enjoy it	Would like to improve
Horseback riding									
Karate/Kung fu									
Lacrosse									
Racquetball									
Running									
Scuba diving									
Self-defense									
Skating—ice									
Skating—roller									
Archery									
Skiing—water									
Skiing—snow									
Soccer									
Tennis									
Track & Field									

Self-Report (Cont.)

Achievement and Play

I am . . .

	A pro	Varsity level	Above average	Average	Below average	Poor	Never did it	Enjoy it	Would like to improve
Volleyball									
Weight training									
Wrestling									
Yoga									
Other: _____									

ness level, success, or failure. Research has suggested four possibilities, especially for older kids: ability, effort, luck, or task difficulty. Their answers provide an opportunity to focus students' attention on setting goals related to ability, effort improvement, or task difficulty and to shift their attention from luck to effort. Journals and counseling days can be useful here.

Self-Report #2

| Rate the following | VI = very important | LI = little importance |
| | SI = somewhat important | NI = no importance |

How important are the following to you?

performing well	VI	SI	LI	NI
having a good-looking body	VI	SI	LI	NI
others' image of me	VI	SI	LI	NI
being a member of a group	VI	SI	LI	NI
enjoying activity	VI	SI	LI	NI
being liked	VI	SI	LI	NI
developing my abilities	VI	SI	LI	NI
my safety	VI	SI	LI	NI
my image of myself	VI	SI	LI	NI
my overall fitness	VI	SI	LI	NI
my arm strength	VI	SI	LI	NI
my stomach strength	VI	SI	LI	NI
my leg strength	VI	SI	LI	NI
my flexibility	VI	SI	LI	NI
my cardiovascular endurance	VI	SI	LI	NI
my ability to stand pain	VI	SI	LI	NI
my coordination	VI	SI	LI	NI
my femininity/masculinity	VI	SI	LI	NI
my health	VI	SI	LI	NI

Self-Report #2 (Cont.)

Rank what is most important to you about your body. Place a "1" by the most important, a "2" by the next most important, and so on.

_____ How I look

_____ Performing well

_____ Health

A. *Muscle Strength*

    a. *I* see myself as:

        Having very strong muscles   Weak

5	4	3	2	1

    b. *Others* see me as being:

        Muscular   Soft

5	4	3	2	1

    c. Being strong is:

        Important enough to work toward on my *own* time.
        Important enough to work toward during *class* time.
        Great if it comes without any work.
        Of little importance.
        Of no importance.

B. *Weight or % Body Fat*

    a. *I* see myself as:

        Perfect
        Only a little over- or underweight.
        Greatly over- or underweight.

    b. *Others* see me as being:

        Perfect
        Only a little over- or underweight.
        Greatly over- or underweight.

Self-Report # 2 (Cont.)

c. Being the right % body fat is:

    Important enough to work toward on my *own* time.

    Important enough to work toward during *class* time.

    Great if it comes without any work.

    Of little importance.

    Of no importance.

C. *Cardiovascular Fitness*

a. *I* see myself as:

    Having C.V. fitness.   Having very poor C.V. fitness.

    5   4   3   2   1

b. *Others* see me as:

    Having great C.V. fitness.   Having very poor C.V. fitness.

    5   4   3   2   1

c. Having a high level of C.V. fitness is:

    Important enough to work toward on my *own* time.

    Important enough to work toward during *class* time.

    Great if it comes without any work.

    Of little importance.

    Of no importance.

D. *Flexibility*

a. *I* see myself as being:

    Flexible as a rubber band.   Flexible as a piece of licorice
                                  on a cold winter's day.

    5   4   3   2   1

Self-Report # 2 (Cont.)

b. *Others* see me as:

Flexible as a rubber band.   Flexible as a piece of licorice
                                          on a cold winter's day.

    5   4   3   2   1

c. Being flexible is:

Important enough to work toward on my *own* time.
Important enough to work toward during *class* time.
Great if it comes without any work.
Of little importance.
Of no importance.

E. *Muscle Endurance*

a. *I* see my level of muscle endurance as being:

Very good. I've got great   Very poor. Can barely hold
"staying" power.   myself up for a whole day.

    5   4   3   2   1

b. *Others* see my level of muscle endurance as being:

Very good. I've got great   Very poor. Can barely hold
"staying" power.   myself up for a whole day.

    5   4   3   2   1

c. Having a good level of muscle endurance is:

Important enough to work toward on my *own* time.
Important enough to work toward during *class* time.
Great if it comes without any work.
Of little importance.
Of no importance.

SPECIFIC STRATEGIES

CHOICES

At Level II, choices were introduced to give students a sense of
ownership in the program as well as to provide options for those
who would be excluded or intimidated otherwise. The introduc-
tion of limited options at Level III encourages students to become
responsible in two ways: first, for their choices, and second, to
stay on task at their choice without direct instructional supervision. Having different activities is one kind of option (e.g., "floor
hockey on this side, tumbling on the other"). Different intensity
is another (e.g., "those of you who want to play a highly competitive game go to that net, the others over here"). Physical activities can meet many different needs: play, achievement,
health, appearance, and so on. You might suggest: "Those who
want to get into their bodies today can take some laps around
the gym; those who want to improve their kicking skills can start
that kicking drill we did yesterday." In organized sport, time can
be set aside for students to work on specific problem areas such
as fielding, throwing, or hitting.

Mark Reznick, an elementary school teacher, reports his surprise at his students' response to choices:

> I picked six activities that we had learned during the year already and told the kids to pick one and do it for the entire time. They had to either play a game or work on the skills of that activity depending on the numbers that were involved in it. Lastly, I said that you couldn't switch from one activity to another upon impulse. They had to do just that one activity. I thought at the time that no way would this work for me. I tried it anyway. This strategy worked beautifully. These are some of my observations: Some girls who I thought disliked basketball joined some boys and played a four on four game; one boy, by himself, found a wall and practiced his soccer skills against it; several kids made variations of the game they were involved with; less than three in every class were actually trying to avoid the task. I was very pleased with this group of kids. I'm now in my second week of doing this strategy and may continue for at least another week.

GRADUALLY INCREASING RESPONSIBILITIES

Gradually widening the range of responsibility is a related strategy. Both options and time can be limited at first and then gradually loosened. The options can be gradually increased so that when students are told to warm-up or overload their bodies or work on a skill, they can choose from a number of activities. At first perhaps only a couple of options should be available. When students demonstrate responsibility in choosing and carrying out an option, the options can be increased. Time can be limited to 15 minutes one day in the week or 5 minutes at the end of some class periods and then gradually increased. Pam Yoder begins her loosening process by organizing a variety of stations, each with a different task and each with a sign-up sheet to be signed when the task is completed. Another idea is to permit students to do their own warm-up after they have experienced the teacher's warm-up routine. If they demonstrate self-responsibility, they can be given more choices and perhaps more time to carry out their choices. Students can be required to earn the right to make choices by first demonstrating some level of responsibility (the reward system idea). That way only those students who are willing and able to work on their own get the privilege of doing so; others can be instructed as a group by the teacher.

If you try any of this and feel as if you are losing control, you may be operating outside your comfort zone or beyond your "chaos level." It is really important not to get so far outside your comfort zone that you become ineffective, so take it slowly and don't be afraid to take a step back and regroup. On the other hand, nothing new is easy, so don't give up too quickly. Instead, take a step back and analyze; then make a plan to try again (your self-responsibility!).

Individualized instruction strategies that range from the very loose to the very structured help students experience self-responsibility. Several books explain these strategies in some detail (Mosston, 1981; AAHPER, 1976). Here are some examples.

TASK CARDS

A task card, either hung on the wall or handed out on a ditto (to be stuffed into the waist band or a sock), describes in detail a progression from the very simple to the very difficult. In throwing, for example, the first step might be to place one's feet correctly. The last step might be to hit a small target five times in a row. This last task should be made to challenge professional athletes. Task cards can be made for all kinds of skills including team sport skills such as dribbling or serving. Each card becomes in effect an assistant teacher or coach. Short strategy quizzes on a table in the corner can also be used to test knowledge progression.

A variation of the task card concept is to provide learning booklets so that each student can work and play at his/her own pace. Karyn Hartinger has created seven of these booklets for her low socioeconomic elementary school kids. She talks to them about choosing, then introduces the booklets. Kids who complete a booklet can become helpers; those who can't stay on task are given direct instruction by Karyn. All students are asked to reflect on their experiences with the booklets each day. Here are some samples.

Jumping Rope

Jumping Rope

Choose a rope for your size.   ____ Completed
(Hold the ends of the rope and
stand on the rope. The handles
should reach between your
waist and under your arms.)

Practice single time—one jump   ____ Completed
with one turn of the rope.

Practice double time—two jumps   ____ Completed
to one turn of the rope.

Using the material in the gym   Stunt _____   ____ Completed
library, try different stunts.
Have a partner check to see if
you have executed the stunt   Stunt _____   ____ Completed
correctly.

Routine

Routine   *My Own Routine*

                                        ____ I designed a jump rope routine.

Choose a short routine from the   ____ I demonstrated this routine.
jump rope file in the PE office. This
must be executed with music.

_____
          Name of Routine

_____
          Name of Music

Performed in front of Mrs. Hartinger.

Partner Rope Skipping

Partner Rope Skipping

List the stunts you can do with a partner.

Jump Roping With Equipment

List the activities you can do while jumping rope (e.g., tinikling, balance beam, etc.).

Wall Ball

Wall Ball (lead up to racquetball)

Objective: To hit the ball against the wall so the opponent will not be able to return the ball.

Rules:
1) Use an 8½" rubber ball.

2) You score only when you serve.

3) The ball may be hit after one bounce or before the bounce.

4) You must hit the wall first after striking the ball.

5) To serve you bounce ball in area and then strike it.

Practice

Practice hitting the ball to the wall. Allow only one bounce after it hits the wall.

____ I can hit the ball against the wall 10 times without missing using my right hand.

____ I can hit the ball against the wall 10 times without missing using my left hand.

____ I can hit the ball against the wall 10 times without missing using either hand.

Wall Ball (Cont.)

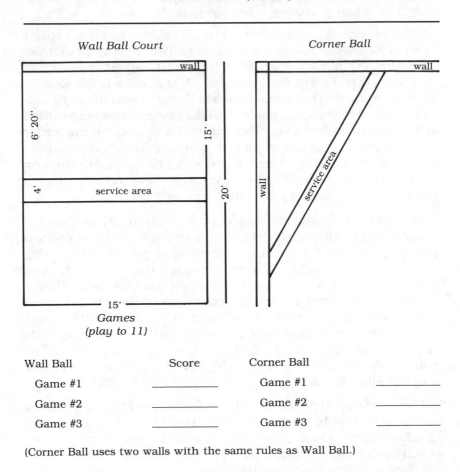

Wall Ball Court   *Corner Ball*

Games
(play to 11)

Wall Ball	Score	Corner Ball	
Game #1	_____	Game #1	_____
Game #2	_____	Game #2	_____
Game #3	_____	Game #3	_____

(Corner Ball uses two walls with the same rules as Wall Ball.)

CONTRACTS

One way to get students to set individual goals and work on them is to make an agreement or contract with each student. Student goals should be based on their self-evaluations and they must have a sufficient concept base to carry out their goals. Students who have difficulty staying on task can be "remanded" to a station where tasks are controlled by the teacher (and supervised either by the teacher or a student leader) until they can set and work on individual goals. A reward system sometimes helps get students on task and keep them there until they become intrinsically motivated to work on their own.

Contracts can be verbal or written. Verbal contracts are easier to initiate although some dialog will usually be necessary to make sure that the students' goals reflect their self-evaluations and that they have a sufficient concept base. A clipboard helps to keep track of promises that students make; a wall chart offers the advantage of visible commitments. When I coached a group of high school wrestlers (Hellison, 1983), I would debrief each wrestler as soon after his match as he was able to concentrate. I would ask what went right and wrong and what he needed to work on next week at practice. Then we would devise a plan and during the week I'd try to help him stay with it.

Written contracts which students carry with them have the advantages of requiring students to clearly specify their goals, a plan to reach their goals, and sometimes a plan for evaluating their progress. Possible disadvantages are that it takes time to write the contracts and keep track of all the paperwork. Some teachers have required students to write contracts outside of class (homework!) if they want the privilege of working on their own. Most teachers who have been successful with written contracts require students to keep track of their own paperwork. The penalty for losing a contract is the loss of privilege of working on individual goals.

I and several other teachers have found working on personal goals to be highly motivating for most kids. However, some teachers have experienced difficulty with student motivation when contracts are introduced. The students don't seem to care, or they would rather do what their friends do. Or, as Frank O'Toole reports, they are conditioned to do what's expected of them instead of creating their own expectations. Although some teachers would love to have Frank's students, these kinds of student attitudes interfere with the development of self-responsibility. My usual response to these kinds of problems is that the stage hasn't been sufficiently set and/or the self-reflection process hasn't been thorough enough (or perhaps hasn't been taken seriously by the students). They just aren't ready for contracts yet. Those who are can go ahead; those who aren't need more preparation.

Dialog can help in the evaluation process. I'll never forget when Beth checked "lose weight" as her goal, then made a plan to play with her friends. When I questioned her, she said, "But I don't want to run," indicating that she knew the concept of exercise for weight control. I just told her to change her plan to running or change her goal to playing with friends. Beth: "But I want to lose weight." Me: "Then change your plan." Beth: "Could I do both?" Me: "Write it up." She did—a combined plan of running and trampoline (with her friends). A week later—Beth: "Do I have to run today?" Me: "It's your plan—change it." Beth: "I have to run." The same year Valerie came to complain that I hadn't told her the time, causing her to be late. "Who's in charge of you?" I asked. "Me," she responded, and walked away smiling.

Written contracts can be as creative as the teacher is. My latest idea has been to require all students to be an "expert" in something. They can choose from performance, knowledge, or teaching skill in a specific sport or an aspect of fitness, or administrative leadership in some aspect of the class. They are required to select one of these areas and to specify the exact content they are going to master. They select their own definition of mastery: excellence compared to others (e.g., top 10%), improvement (e.g., pre- and posttesting), or uniqueness (no one else does this). Then they make a plan, carry it out and, finally, share their results with other students (this last being a Level IV activity).

Carrying out contracts can test the teacher's chaos level. Most teachers who use contracts designate at the most 2 days a week for working on and carrying out contracts. Even 15 minutes a week would give students some experience in this kind of self-responsibility.

I know teachers who have used contracts with first graders! And with very poor readers and writers in all grades. Here are specific examples to give you some ideas of what contracts can look like. Again, teacher creativity to fit individual situations is crucial.

The "Learning Plan for Fitness" was created by Gary Kuney to enable his fourth- through eighth-grade students to assess their skills (reflection time), set goals, and make choices. The next three contracts were developed by Gayle MacDonald for use in an inner-city high school. They progressively give students permission to work on their own and make choices, beginning with very structured contracts (numbered one) and moving toward more self-responsibility (in contracts two and three). The "Contract Learning Unit" was created by Peter Teppler as a special unit of excellence for physical education students who had completed ninth grade physical education. Students plan their own unit and help to grade themselves.

Learning Plan for Fitness

Name _____

Grade _____

Rate your present skill.

pro	excellent	very good	good	ok	so so	could be better	I do not care

Where would you like to be?

pro	excellent	very good	good	ok	so so	could be better	I do not care

Grouping I want to be in!

Jog and giggle _____   Jog and compete _____

1. All students will participate in lecture and skills development drills.

2. Each student must select 4 goals or 1 lab and 2 goals.

   Goal A: Book report on skill _____

   Goal B: Pass test on rules _____

   Goal C: Work with others in positive manner _____

   Goal D: Improve skills _____

   Goal E: Give written report on history _____

   Goal F: Give it your best shot _____

   Goal G: Adhere to safety rules _____

   Lab A: Physiology of exercise lab _____

   Lab B: Kinesiology _____

take it in stride

I agree
to fill this
learning plan

_____
student

_____
witness:
Mr. Kuney

WHAT A WINNER!

Contract 1A

Name _____

Flexibility

Directions: You do this entire contract for 6 days. As you do each exercise check it off. Do each stretch very slowly, holding it for at least 3 full breaths, relax, then repeat it again. To progress to the next contract you must pass a written fitness knowledge test.

Exercise	*How Much*	*Dates*
1. Neck rotations		
2. Shoulder rotations		
3. Mountain		
4. Forward hanging		
5. Twisting		
6. Side bends		
7. Shooting bow		
8. Straddle stretch		
9. Butterfly		
10. Relaxation	2-3 minutes	
11. Cat		
12. Bow		
13. Long sit		
14. Shoulder stand	1-2 minutes	
15. Plough	1 minute	
16. Arch-up	30 seconds	
17. Child's pose		
18. Relaxation	2-3 mintues	

Contract 1B

Muscular Endurance

Muscular Endurance is the ability of a muscle to repeat an action many times (as in doing many sit-ups, etc.). To train for muscular endurance you would lift light weights many times. You will do this contract for 6 days. As you do each exercise either check it off, record the amount of weight you used, or the number or repetitions accomplished. Except for stretching, you may do the remainder of the workout in any order. To progress to the next contract you must pass a written fitness knowledge test.

Exercise	*How Much*	*Dates*
1. Warm up	1st 5 minutes	
2. Bench press	2 sets of 10-15	
3. Leg press	2 × 10-15	
4. Pull-downs	2 × 10-15	
5. Leg extensions	2 × 10-15	
6. Curls	2 × 10-15	
7. Leg curls	2 × 10-15	
8. Push-ups	As many as possible	
9. Sit-ups	20-40	
10. Jump rope	2 × 1 minute	
11. Easy jogging warm-down	1 lap	
12. Stretching	Last 5 minutes	

Cardiovascular Endurance

Directions: Cardiovascular endurance is the ability of the heart to work hard over a long period of time. To increase your cardiovascular endurance you must have your heart rate at 150 beats/minute for 15 minutes 3 times a week.

Contract 1C

You will do this contract for 6 days. Choose one of the following options and do ALL of it (you may do a different option each time). To progress to the next contract you must pass a written fitness knowledge test.

Dates

Option 1 (in the gym)
1. Warm up—first 5 min.
2. 15-minute jog
3. Stretching—last 5 min.

Option 2 (in the gym)
1. Warm up—first 5 min.
2. 10-minute jog
3. 3 × 1-minute jump rope
4. Stretching—last 5 min.

Option 3 (on the track)
1. Warm up—first 5 min.
2. Jog 2 laps
3. Walk ½ lap
4. Jog 1 lap
5. Walk ½ lap
6. Jog 1 lap
7. Walk ½ lap
8. Stretching—last 5 min.

Option 4 (on the track)
1. Warm up—first 5 min.
2. Jog 6-8 laps
3. Walk 1 lap
4. Stretching—last 5 min.

Option 4

You negotiate something with me.

Contract 2

Name _____

Directions: Choose one or more of the following goals. Only pick goals you are sincere about working on.

1. _____ Cardiovascular endurance   6. _____ Losing weight

2. _____ Muscular endurance   7. _____ Gaining weight

3. _____ Strength   8. _____ Toning muscles

4. _____ Flexibility   9. _____ Relaxation

5. _____ Other _____   10. _____ Other _____

Based on these goals, write a fitness contract that will last for 25-30 minutes.

Exercise	How Much	For Which Goal	Dates
1.			
2.			
3.			
4.			
5.			
6.			
7.			
8.			
9.			
10.			
11.			
12.			

Contract 3

Name _____ Dates _____

You may now divide your time into two 15-minute segments and include a sport of your choice. In the circle to the right, fill in the fitness activities and sport you wish to get better at.

Fitness(15 min.)

Skill/Play
(15 min.)

Examples:

    Fitness—stretch 5 min., jog 10 min.

    Skill & Play—develop jumpshot, play basketball

I. Fitness

          What?   Where?   Why?

II. Skill and/or Play

          What?   Where?   Why?

Contract 3 (Cont.)

Remember the three things you must do to learn a new skill or get better at an old one:

1. Get a picture of it in your mind's eye.

2. Practice the action over and over again.

3. Get feedback from someone on what you're doing right and wrong.

   I.   What skill will I see you working on?

  II. How should it look if you're doing it right?

III. How are you going to practice it?

IV. What feedback did you get about what you were doing right or wrong?

Contract Learning Unit

What's It All About

The purpose of this unit is to give you, the student, an opportunity to zero in on an activity that you feel very good about doing and one that you want to become more proficient at. Because you are taking Physical Education 20 *or* 30, it is felt that you must be keenly interested in pursuing a PE related occupation or at least adopting a personal life style that is rooted in physical activity and physical fitness.

Many of the things we learn (if not most) do not come *directly* from teachers. It is also unrealistic to expect one teacher in any area (math, social studies, or sciences) to know every detail of that subject. Some of you who have been taking flute lessons since Grade 3 will know more about the flute specifically than your music teacher who knows music in general terms but who is really into piano personally.

So, there will be times when you are interested in something and you must "take charge" of your own learning. *You* must decide on the what, how, where, when, and whys of your learning process. This contract unit will allow and help you make these kinds of decisions about yourself.

The PE 20 students must choose activities that can be done within the school, but consideration will be given to out-of-school activities (i.e., swimming, equestrian pursuits, ski jumping, etc.).

You can work by yourself, with a partner, or in a group up to a maximum of four, but each person must complete a written unit.

Evaluation

Evaluation

The unit mark will be composed of 50% teacher evaluation and 50% student evaluation.

Self-Evaluation _____ %

I feel I deserve the above mark for the following reasons:

1)

2)

Evaluation (Cont.)

3)

4)

Teacher Evaluation _____ %

The above mark is assigned for the following reasons:

1)

2)

3)

4)

5)

Final Grade Assigned: _____ %

Date _____ Student signature _____

Teacher signature _____

Read carefully the breakdown of marks for the contract learning unit. Evaluate your unit on the following criteria and decide where you fit in in the scale of marks.

1) Select the *word* grade (excellent, very good, good, satisfactory, incomplete) as to where you feel you fit in.

2) Select a percent grade within the range given. If you feel you have met all the requirements of grade, you should assign yourself a grade within the upper range.

   If you have not met all of the requirements of the grade, your mark should be within the lower range.

Excellent: 85-100%

- Used a variety of resources (people, materials, situations).
- Incorporated different learning techniques in your unit.
- Time was well organized.
- Worked specifically in developing your skills, strategies, and knowledge indicated in the contract plan.
- Drills/exercises, activities were well explained and written out in each daily contract plan.
- Post-practice entries were made after each activity session.
- Felt the experience was extremely rewarding to you—in that you gained new knowledge and skills related to the activity of your choosing.
- You were capable of handling your learning experience.
- You could now be responsible to "take charge" of your learning in many different activities and consider it to be a competent level of mastery.
- You can do skills and execute strategies that you were not able to do before the unit.

Evaluation (Cont.)

Very Good: 75-85%

- Experience was valuable in that you did gain new knowledge and skills in the area of your choosing.
- Time was fairly well organized but had a bit of time left that was not planned (i.e., free time—play time).
- Drills and exercises were written out and explained in the contract plan.
- Post-practice entries were made after each activity session.
- The experience of self-responsibility in the learning of the skills/strategies was beneficial to you, you are capable of handling "learning" in this kind of situation at a competent level.
- Used a few different techniques and incorporated them into your learning activities.
- Used a variety of different resource material.

Good: 65-75%

- You were capable of handling the learning of new skills and knowledge to a limited extent. You took charge of your learning at a very basic level of knowledge and skill. You did not go into any detail on advanced skills and strategies even though you could have. Basically stayed on same skills and level of knowledge throughout the entire unit.
- Used a few different sources for resources.
- Used basically similar learning techniques throughout the unit.
- Drills and exercises were briefly summarized each day—not in any detail.
- Time was well used—but perhaps you didn't pursue the *learning* for the entire contract unit.
- Covered the activity to an adequate degree.

Satisfactory: 50-65%

- Did use the time to participate in an activity. The activity consisted of basically practicing skills that you could already do.
- Did not increase your knowledge or skill level of the activity but worked at the level already at.
- Used a limited source of resource information. Each lesson was repetitive and structured similar to the previous one.
- Did not research into your subject to any great extent.
- Did not use the idea of the contract learning (excellence unit) to its maximum benefit.
- Did not get involved in any research into more *advanced* strategies or knowledge.
- Brief summary of what you did each session was written in your contract unit daily. No details of your drills or class were written in.
- Would have preferred if someone else had taken charge of your learning experience in the unit (teacher, instructor).

Incomplete: 50%

- Did not complete the necessary requirement of the unit.

Personal Skills Inventory

---

1. The sport or activity I want to improve or get better at is:

2. The value of this activity or the reasons for getting proficient at it are as follows:

   a)

   b)

   c)

   d)

3. Personal skills inventory: (What can I do now!) You can do this by yourself, with a coach, with a partner who is familiar with your performance, or with an opponent you play against. This involves taking stock of what you can do and how well you can do the skills within the sport or activity you have chosen. Identify each skill and rate yourself.

   #1) Know about the skill but do not know how to do it well, or can just barely do it.

   #2) Can do the skill at an average skill level, but realize there is room for lots of improvement.

   #3) Can do the skill very well. The only improvements are minute, fine-tuning things.

4. What skills, strategies, or concepts do you hope to master during the contract unit? What are your goals and objectives? Be very specific. This information should come from the Personal Skills Inventory section.

Skill: Level you aspire to
                                                finish at (#1, #2, #3)

Personal Skills Inventory (Cont.)

5. *Resource Materials*

Where will you find the information on how to become better? This may be from books, films, magazines, talking to or watching people who can already do what you are trying to accomplish, and so forth. List your resources. Be very specific.

*Session #*_____

Length of time you practiced for _____ Date you practiced _____

Where you practiced _____

What skills, drills, and techniques do you plan to work on (this must be filled out *before*, not after, the session). Indicate time (minutes) or number of repetitions you intend to work for.

Skill	Drill	Technique	Time

Post-Practice Comments:

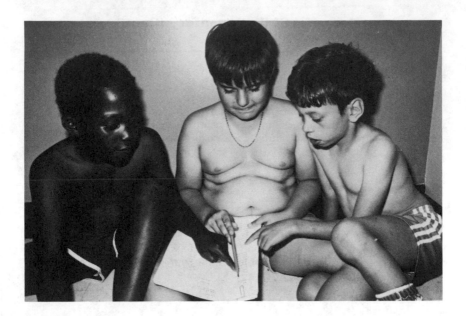

For other contract ideas, see Corbin and Lindsey's *Fitness for Life* (1983, pp. 163-164, 171-172, 175-181) and my *Beyond Balls and Bats* (Hellison, 1978, pp. 74-78). Corbin and Lindsey give detailed, step-by-step guidance in making both exercise and sport contracts based on their conceptual approach. My contracts proved useful in getting problem kids to work on their own.

INSTRUCTIONAL AIDS

Another individualized strategy is to use books, pictures, loop films, and other media to help kids learn on their own. I relied heavily on a gymnastics book to carry me through teaching gymnastics; I was able to obtain enough books so that every three or four kids could share one. I've also used a yoga book to help a student who wanted to learn that subject matter and a kung fu book for three Bruce Lee fanatics. A basketball jump shot loop film helped some would-be NBA stars get their elbows in the right place while I was busy elsewhere. The best book I've seen in this regard is Guthrie's *Be Your Own Coach* (1982). It teaches kids how to coach themselves in youth soccer programs but could be adapted for other sports.

PROBLEM SOLVING

Problem solving and the "open gym" also provide individualized opportunities for students. Problem solving can mean turning the teacher's answer—how to do a skill—into a question, allowing students time to explore alternatives. It takes more time, but students take more responsibility for their work. Problem solving can also mean movement exploration in which students are given open-ended tasks to be solved through movement in any number of ways. An open gym is one in which equipment and space are made available, students are taught safety procedures and then are allowed to dabble, explore, and practice at their own pace as long as they stay busy (and do not violate the first rule). Watch your chaos level if you try this one!

ADAPTING TO SUPERVISION AND FACILITIES PROBLEMS

Both supervision and limited facilities present problems. Most schools have at least somewhat different supervision expectations; this means adjusting the extent of individualization to the setting in addition to one's own guidelines for safety. Lots of activity can go on in one room within view of the teacher. I've had kids set up a volleyball net for bump-set practice in the weight room, run agility drills in a hallway outside the gym, practice karate skills with a mirror in an equipment closet, and so on. Students protest at first; after all, NCAA standards aren't being met! But when faced with the choice of doing their own program (or contract) or doing mine, they quickly find ways to adapt to the limited space.

COPING WITH SPECIFIC NEEDS

Strategies that focus on specific needs can help students work through difficult personal decisions. Bob Blanchette of Calgary has developed a courage unit in gymnastics to help middle-school boys cope with this typical expectation for males in our culture.

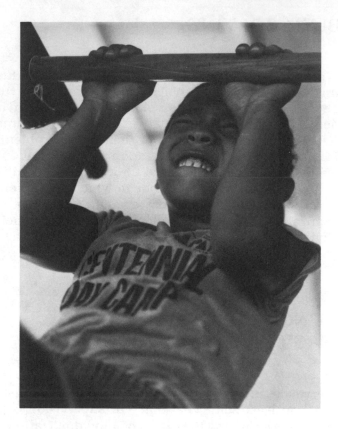

He believes that gymnastics offer many opportunities to confront risky situations, and that encouraging students to express their feelings as they struggle with these situations will help them develop courage—both in gymnastics and in their lives. The workbook he gives them includes both reflection time activities and physical experiences. The following was taken from the workbook:

Teaching Courage Through Gymnastics

A. Definitions:

Courage is the ability to meet the challenge of something you feel is difficult to cope with, or to stand up for a philosophical belief or a truth.

Teaching Courage Through Gymnastics (Cont.)

B. Goal Clarification:

Courage is the tool used to accomplish those things within you that you fear or that you never thought you could do.

C. Self-Evaluation:

The two statements on the right and left indicate two different views on the subject of courage. For example, if you wrote a statement like the one on the right it would indicate that you had some understanding of the concept of courage. If you can write both statements, it is a good indicator that you totally understand the concept of courage.

D. Understanding of Courage:

I have courage if:	*I don't have courage if:*
I try new skills even though I may be afraid or look foolish.	I continually find excuses for myself to avoid trying a new skill in the P.E. program.
I stay home and study for the biology exam even though my friends want me to go out with them.	I go out and party with my friends even though I have an exam the next morning.

E. In the space provided, write in two examples of courage. These examples should reflect both whether you do or do not understand courage. (See examples provided in Section D.)

F. All of us at some time have to do things in the gymnastics program that we are afraid of. In the space provided, write a few skills that you have trouble coping with or have problems doing physically.

G. From the list of skills you have identified, write down the one you feel you could beat or would like to by the end of the course. This should be something you could master or be challenged by.

Teaching Courage Through Gymnastics (Cont.)

H. One of the healthiest signs for self-growth is to meet the challenge set by those obstacles you are most afraid of.

   a) Describe how you felt trying your activity for the first time.

   b) What pitfalls did you have to meet in doing your activity?

   c) What psychological things did you feel while trying to learn your skill, and when you had completed the movement for the first time?

   d) What were the feelings you were experiencing just prior to accomplishing your skill? This will be physiological and deals with the body's changes.

   e) Did you meet the challenge of your particular skill?

               Yes   No   Undecided

   f) If yes: describe your feelings once you finished the movement.

   g) If no: then describe what you could have done differently to help meet this obstacle.

   h) Would you try an activity of this type again? Why? Why not?

My own work with combative activities has been in part an effort to help students reduce their feelings of vulnerability. Some students don't feel vulnerable; others walk around scared much of the time. I have required all students to sit in on a discussion of the purposes of combative activities (i.e., self-protection and learning to survive being hit) and to take a couple of introductory lessons. Those who want to do more are then given opportunities to work with me at an optional station while other students choose other activities or rotate to different stations.

CURRICULUM CONSIDERATIONS

Infusing Level III into the curriculum requires the implementation of four procedures. First, the teacher must include repeated references to students' potential to take charge of themselves. Second, time must be set aside to help students reflect on their needs and interests on a regular basis. Third, time must be set aside each week for students to experiment with making and carrying out their choices. Fourth, some reflection time must be included to evaluate the Level III experiences. The third procedure causes sport and exercise leaders the most anxiety for a number of reasons: the recent emphasis on legal liability for the supervision of students, particularly regarding safety; insufficient space and equipment to individualize; and the difficulty many students have in staying on task without direct supervision. If you decide to implement Level III, the following guidelines can help:

GO SLOWLY

Go very slowly. Set aside a few minutes each week for a fairly specific task, for example stretching without a teacher. Then evaluate the results and proceed from there.

A cautionary note: In one setting I overemphasized Level III. Because this level is so difficult to implement, I spent most of my time and energy here. As a result, students felt very much in charge of themselves—more than they actually were—but their Level IV attitudes and actions were minimal except with close friends. Going slowly and evaluating as you go not only prevents disaster but also lessens the chance of getting carried away!

DON'T EXCEED YOUR OWN LIMITS

Never go beyond your own chaos level! We all have our own limits beyond which we feel out of control. Push your limits but don't exceed them.

ESTABLISH A PROGRESSION

Establish a progression. If students can do the stretching exercises they were taught without direct leadership, allow them to choose the stretching exercises that they want to do. If they can handle that, perhaps they are ready to select some fitness goals to carry out during the first few minutes of class. If they can handle that, perhaps one day a week they can plan and do their own program. And so on.

PLAN YOUR PAPERWORK

Don't do written contracts if you can't stand the paperwork; but if this approach makes sense to you, require your students to assume much of the responsibility for the paperwork (e.g., doing it right, hanging onto the contracts, and so on). If they lose the papers, they lose their privileges (they don't lose $10 bills, and they won't lose the paperwork if it is worth something to them!).

USE TEACHER TALK
AND SELF-REFLECTION

Connect your teacher talk and reflection time to opportunities to make and carry out choices.

INDIVIDUALIZATION

Nowhere is the difference in each individual's entry level and development more visible than at Level III. Some kids can plan and work alone for a long time. Some can do it for a short time before their interest wanes. Some can plan but can't implement without a support group. (One Level IV strategy is to form support groups of students who have the same goals.) Some can plan and carry out their plans if you help them. Some seem unable or unwilling to plan or implement even with your help. Two guidelines can help the individualization process if you decide to implement Level III:

1. Help each student take a tiny step forward in self-responsibility. When I individualized a weight training unit, Gene said he couldn't do it and wanted me to lead him through a routine. I asked him if he knew what exercises he wanted to do; he said yes and listed them. I asked if he knew how much weight and repetitions he needed to do; he said yes and told me. I said "Go do this first exercise;" he did and reported back. I gave him the second exercise on his list to do, and off he went. Gene worked well this way; he could be more responsible than he thought, but less than I had required of everyone. Another time when students were developing their own physical education plans, Maurice could not read and write very well, so I wrote his contract for him. He was the consultant to his own plan rather than the other way around. He did a good job of carrying out his contract.

2. Don't punish the whole group if some kids can't set goals or if they stray off task. Those specific kids need the help, not everyone. One of my trainees spent 10 minutes lecturing his inner-city class on being more responsible, then let them all go back to their individual programs. He admitted that over half the kids didn't need the lecture and at least five weren't ready to do their own program even with the lecture!

CONCLUSION

Being at Level III means more than being under control and more than being involved under the teacher's supervision. It means taking responsibility for as much of one's attitudes and actions as circumstances will allow, and accepting the results without blaming others. Self-responsibility also means making thoughtful choices, being able to work without supervision, and setting and carrying out goals that will help to give life more meaning and will give satisfying answers to the identity question "Who am I?" Level III, self-responsibility, is a lifetime process which requires the ability to laugh at oneself and to be spontaneous while being goal-oriented. This chapter has described a number of guidelines, interaction strategies, and implementation ideas that you can consider for your specific situation. Once this Level III process is under way and students feel that they are beginning to have some control over the direction of their lives, they can then begin to reach out to others and experience Level IV.

CHAPTER 6

CARING STRATEGIES
(LEVEL IV)

Level I attempts to reduce interference with the rights of others, Level II to encourage meaningful involvement, and Level III to improve responsible decision-making toward a more integrated, stable identity. If these goals are met, to what extent will the current confusion, insecurity, isolation, and alienation be reduced? And to what extent will the large, impersonal nature of many schools be counteracted? Levels II and III help in the development of personal stability, and Level I helps social stability by protecting our rights against infringement. However, if we really want to improve social stability, we will need to commit ourselves to others. This is no upstart value; our society has always valued caring and has encouraged voluntary humanitarian concerns despite a parallel tradition of individualism and competition. Caring is a value that taps an intrinsic impulse; we simply need each other. We need affection, affiliation, help, love, and we always have. It's just that we need these qualities more in today's world.

DEVELOPMENTAL LEVEL IV

Caring refers to extending one's sense of responsibility beyond one's self to others. Perhaps it is the most anyone can do for others. Caring is also an important social and personal need; most people need others to care about them. Students who care are more cooperative, are more interested in collaborating on mutual goals, and are more supportive of each other by being a friend or by being "there" when needed. Students who care help others to overcome obstacles without requiring favors in return ("I'll do this for you if you do that for me"). They respect the other person intrinsically so that help is not thrust upon the other whether or not he/she wants it.

The full development of caring requires that students acquire a sense of purpose in life that extends beyond personal involvement and development to a commitment to bettering the world (Sheehy, 1981). "It is essential to the well-being of an individual and society to progress from concern for self to concern for others to concern for all" (Craig, 1982). A sense of purpose larger than self will help reduce the egocentered impact of winning and losing, of going from "hero to zero" (Orlick, 1980) as a former athlete, of the arrogance that may result from special treatment often accorded a talented athlete. It helps students to "see life large" (Robert Frost), to place their successes and failures in a wider, less egocentric context.

A caring continuum might look like this:

Less				*More*
Cooperation	Part of someone's support system	Concern for others beyond friends	Helping	Sense of purpose beyond self

Caring has been placed at Level IV due to the work of a number of scholars who argue that the self must be taken care of first, that we must meet some of our own needs before we can reach out very far or very often to others. The development of a strong, stable, integrated identity permits us to care. However, agreement on this point is by no means complete. In our culture, the developmental sequence could well be gender specific; or perhaps such scholars as Maslow (1970), Bronfenbrenner (1980), and Jurkovic and Selman (1980) who have argued one way or another that caring does not require self-development could be right. I'm not persuaded, but I do want to recognize the tentative basis for placing caring at Level IV.

A grim seriousness sometimes accompanies caring, especially when it is seen as the central purpose for being. Caring is not a solo act; caring people need time for self-maintenance and self-development, time to grow, to celebrate, and to rest and recuperate. It also helps to have a sense of humor about the stumbling and fumbling usually associated with trying to make things better, and sometimes even about the world itself.

INTERACTION STRATEGIES

TEACHER TALK

Teacher talk can help students to interact with Level IV in the following ways:

EMPHASIZE CARING

Caring is Level IV in the developmental levels; therefore, talks about the levels emphasize caring as an advanced quality and hopefully give students a framework for operating in the gym and elsewhere. Teachable moments will occur in which students do or do not support and help each other. I've found that students listen and understand the levels better in these situations, but it takes practice to integrate them in a meaningful manner. When I first got started, I would often respond to those incidents in traditional ways—by ignoring or yelling—even though I was teaching the awareness levels to them at other times.

   Linda Lachey-Helms reports this incident after teaching Level IV in her high school floor hockey unit:

> While the puck was lost in the bleachers and part of the class was looking for it, a really exciting event took place. I looked to one end of the gym and there was one of the students trying to help the other team's goalie by kneeling down and giving him some tips on how to move his stick on the floor. The student didn't have anything to gain by helping the other team's goalie so I called him over and told him how very nice I thought his gesture was. He looked at me and said that he was just checking out how Level IV felt and that he decided it felt pretty good.

Talks about a sense of purpose beyond one's self take on more meaning if they begin with the impact of winning and losing, of "looking good" in the gym, of being an athletic hero-heroine. Eventually, these ups and downs can be placed within larger perspective.

TRANSFER OUTSIDE THE GYM

Teacher talk can remind students to transfer caring from the gym to the rest of life, that the gym is just one part of the larger picture.

MODELING (BEING)

Modeling is a subtle but powerful strategy in the promotion of caring attitudes and behaviors.

MODELING CARING

Teachers are helping professionals; they must live this role and students must feel it. Students don't have to be loved—some of them are hard to love; but teachers do have to love the act of caring. It must truly be what they are there for.

MODELING SENSE OF HUMOR

It really helps to have a sense of humor, to be able to make fun of one's self in a light, nondeprecating way. A large part of being human is stumbling and struggling; to be able to laugh a little at one's own stumbling and struggling acknowledges this humanness and may even open the door to the caring process. If I don't take myself too seriously, perhaps I can find some time for others in my life.

MODELING LEVEL IV NEEDS

All of us have a support system; we teachers need to let students know this (without hitting them over the head about our personal lives, of course). It is important that they don't get the idea that their teacher sleeps in the gym or that he/she is alive only to take care of them. Teachers have needs too, and one of them—an important one—is to be loved.

REINFORCEMENT

Reinforcement strategies can help to emphasize Level IV.

PRAISE

Specific and genuine praise is an important reinforcer in the development of caring. As teachers, we have to look for it just as we look for motor skill or fitness improvement.

AWARDS

Awards for best helper, leader, support person, and so on help to reinforce the importance of helping. Helping is not so easily measured as batting averages, mile times, and other objective statistics.

REWARDS

Gary Kuney reports some success in his elementary classes by giving points to those kids who, in his judgment, show empathy or perspective-taking (putting themselves in others' gym shoes). The points are traded in for a movie and popcorn at the end of the year.

CONTRACT CRITERIA

I have included helping behaviors as one of the criteria for earning an advanced contract (Hellison, 1978). Students could help by showing a new student how the program works, by helping another student fill out a contract, or by helping another student learn or practice a skill.

STUDENT-TO-STUDENT REINFORCEMENT

Another approach is to encourage students to reinforce each other. Bonnie Gleason Burke wrote the following about her reinforcement program for young kids.

Warm Fuzzies are good strokes which give us warm feelings, feelings of being OK, of being loved. Cold Pricklies are strokes which feel bad.

By giving Warm Fuzzies, good strokes to others, you can feel good too. Give Warm Fuzzies by doing something nice for someone. I explain this to the children and then teach them the words to the Warm Fuzzy song. We spend the last few minutes of class learning the song and giving Warm Fuzzies.

Once the concept is learned I place a small box full of puff-like cotton balls on a table in the corner of the gym. I explain to the kids that sometimes it's hard to talk to someone who you know needs some Warm Fuzzies. If they see a student during their class who looks like he needs some extra attention, they can go and take a Warm Fuzzy out of the box and give it to another child. The kids know what this means. Some kids can just say to others verbally what's needed; others can't. This gives them the option.

REFLECTION TIME

The same kinds of reflection time experiences can be used for caring as for the other goals. It is perhaps even more important for this goal, because ethical reflection is mentioned in some of the literature as a factor in the development of conscience. Perhaps both Level I, self-control, and Level IV, caring, require the development of some guilt! (We middle-class adults could use a little less.) In addition, these strategies might help:

Students could be asked to check the place they occupy on a continuum of caring attitudes and acts, from cooperation on one end to a sense of purpose and commitment beyond self on the other.

| Cooperation | Part of someone's support system | Concern for others beyond friends | Helping | Sense of purpose beyond self |

It might help students' perspective to ask them to what extent being an athlete or nonathlete or winning or losing dominates their life. Is it more important to be successful than to help someone? What about in 10 years? In 30 years?

Bonnie Gleason Burke described her reflection time for young kids as follows:

I've used six different areas that children might relate to to express their feelings. At the end of class the children pick one slip of paper which best describes how they felt about themselves and class for the day. They place the slip of paper in a box labeled—HOW ARE YOU TODAY!!
I go through the slips of paper and try to get an idea of where the class was "on a whole" for the day. The six areas are:

1. I got my feelings hurt today.

2. I hurt someone's feelings today.

3. I helped a friend.

4. I had fun today.

5. I cooperated today.

6. I made a new friend today.

For children to pick one of these makes them become aware of how they emotionally really handled the day's class.

Peter Teppler uses a "Big Ideas Sheet" with a self-inventory to help his high school students reflect on their caring behavior. He believes that students need to be directly confronted by the notion of caring for others and to be forced to evaluate the extent of caring that they regularly engage in. His students fill out the following evaluation, which is followed by a discussion of caring.

Big Ideas Sheet

A. Goal

Caring

B. Definition of the Goal:

We are not hermits. We look to others to fill many of our emotional, social and physical needs. Likewise, we can fill these needs for others.

C. Reasons for Valuing the Goal:

Realization of the fact that you need other people will help you build ties with others. Other people will value you if you help them in meeting their goals, just as you feel a tie towards anyone that assists or helps to make you feel good.

D. Self-Inventory   (Circle one)

CODE:	5	(Very often)
	4	(Frequently)
	3	(Occasionally)
	2	(Seldom)
	1	(Never)

I understand caring if:			I don't understand caring if:	
I'm quiet when the teacher is talking.			I talk and interfere with others' rights and responsibility to teach.	
5	4	3	2	1
I helped someone recently.			I can't remember the last time I helped someone.	
5	4	3	2	1

Big Ideas Sheet (Cont.)

I let people help me learn new or difficult things in PE and other classes.			I don't let people help me because I'll look weak or inferior to that person.	
5	4	3	2	1
I compliment people on things that they do well.			I never compliment anyone because they'll think they have the one-up on me.	
5	4	3	2	1
I thank people who have helped me.			I don't thank anyone because I'm too tough and cool.	
5	4	3	2	1
I'm humble about the talents I have.			I flaunt my talents and wipe them on others.	
5	4	3	2	1
I shared something with someone recently.			I never share anything because I might not get it back or they might not repay me.	
5	4	3	2	1 1
I stuck up for or found something good about someone everyone else was putting down.			I like getting into a group and tearing someone apart that everyone agrees is a jerk.	
5	4	3	2	1 1
I can accept compliments graciously.			I can't accept compliments because I think they're trying to get something from me.	
5	4	3	2	1

STUDENT SHARING

STUDENT DECISION-MAKING

Student sharing which leads to small- and large-group decision-making can help students learn to cooperate and to develop a sense of community (McNeill, 1982). Students can help to develop rules for the class, safety procedures, and/or sportsmanship

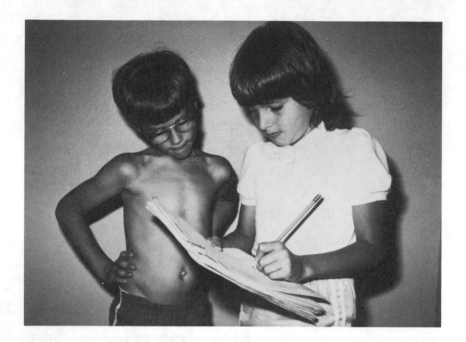

guidelines. Students can be asked for their input or can be given the job of developing the rules and guidelines either with or without the teacher's option to veto their ideas. The development of a class charter (Jones & Jones, 1981, p. 135) may provide a focus for these efforts. So will raising a group issue that "affects everyone in the group to one degree or another" (Lickona, 1982).

Students can also be given the task of planning and carrying out a day's activities. When I tried this in an inner-city high school, my class didn't know what to do. I didn't give them a procedure; the only rule was, whatever activities are agreed upon must be participated in by all students. I asked them to plan for the next four Fridays. A leader finally emerged out of the confusion. He usually led people the wrong way, but he took nominations, heard arguments, and conducted the vote. He didn't get his way, which was to play basketball for all the Fridays, but the students did eventually agree on a plan and they managed to carry it out.

David Holmberg directs a program for 10 students with records of low achievement and high misbehavior at a Portland suburban high school. Together they decided that the class goal would be to climb Mt. Hood at the end of the year. They discussed the criteria for participation in the climb and decided, with David's help, upon three criteria: Each student would have to run 2 miles nonstop with no time limit before the climb; each student would have to work for 20 hours to earn money for equipment (funded by a local agency); and each student would have to sew the equipment (sewing machines were available in class). Part of the school year was spent on working toward this goal. All students but one eventually qualified. Should the one who did not meet the criteria go anyway? David put it to the group with the nonqualifying student present. They decided that he shouldn't, and he didn't. They made the climb, experienced a blizzard, and had to quit a bit short of the summit; yet the students perceived it as a success as evidenced by their celebrations the following days (and weeks).

Pam Yoder uses student sharing with her high school basketball team. They suggest team strengths and weaknesses and help to make a plan for the season.

CREATING NEW GAMES

Students can also be asked to invent new games for everyone to play. My first effort at this involved a third grade class that invented a game in which several students got left out and one little girl got a skinned knee. When we debriefed, the kids who dominated the game gave it a high evaluation. However, when I asked them about the extent of participation and safety, the kids who didn't like the game talked and eventually they all agreed on rule modifications.

Another time, a class of high school students divided into four groups according to their choice to create new games. Two groups—comprising the more compliant and productive kids—immediately created a couple of fun games that we played. A third group was totally nonproductive, and the fourth group, despite our guideline to invent something new and not a variation of a traditional game, created "strip volleyball!" This game was to be played in the wrestling room sitting on the floor with two students holding the net up. Volleyball rules were to be observed with the addition that whenever someone made an error, this person would take off one article of clothing. The team with the smallest pile would be declared the winner! When I and my co-teacher, Liz Nixon, called their bluff, several students declined to participate at first. The kids had so much paraphernalia (earrings, combs, picks, what-have-you) that no one was threatened, and eventually all were playing. However, Eddie came in without a shirt on—he did have a hat—and he was down to his shorts with 2 minutes to go and his friends chanting, "Hit it to Eddie!'' We scooted over to stave off volleyballs, and he survived. . .barely. A visiting teacher observed all of this, to my chagrin, and introduced the game to her kids! Latest reports have several teachers doing it, but the NCAA has yet to publish a rulebook.

SPECIFIC STRATEGIES

COOPERATIVE GAMES

Cooperative games can emphasize achievement of a mutually desired goal. They can range from modifications of traditional games to new games. One modification of a traditional game that I have used requires all players to touch the ball before each shot in basketball. I organized a team of "scrubs" who beat the class hotshots at this game, because the hotshots didn't want to pass the ball and spent the entire game arguing with each other. I

found that the rule had to be structured to really include everyone or else some students would be reduced to the role of touching the ball and getting out of the way. Pam Yoder uses this game with her high school basketball team in practice to emphasize cooperation. Tom Hinton has had success with a new game in which one team tries to place a piece of tape higher on a wall than another team; both cooperation and group decision-making are encouraged. Deta Holcombe has her pregnant and unwed mothers help each other over a high bar as a variation of getting all students over a wall in typical ropes course setups.

In blindfold soccer, students work in pairs: the one who is blindfolded does the kicking while his/her partner gives directions. When I introduced this activity to my inner-city class, one kid ran his partner (and friend) into a goal post and then doubled over with laughter. Needless to say, a fight ensued. This is another example of the need for rules and guidance beyond just introducing the activity. Trust falls ask students to fall from a choice of heights (from standing on the ground to a bench or table) into the arms of other students. Some training is needed to pull this one off, but we have found it to be an effective cooperation activity. Electric wire is a typical initiative game which requires students to escape from a compound surrounded by a high electric fence (rope). Such games and modifications can be taken from sources such as Orlick (1978) and Rohnke (1977) or, with a little innovation, can be created by the teacher.

Other kinds of cooperative activities can be introduced as well, limited only by the teacher's creativity. Tom Hinton has organized an Ethnic Olympics in his inner-city school in which students research, select, and teach activities from different cultures.

LEVEL III SUPPORT GROUPS

Support groups of students with similar goals (thanks to Mark Tager) not only facilitate the implementation and evaluation of individual plans (Level III) but also encourage the development of support systems and concern for others (Level IV) as well. Simply build into the individualized planning process some time for students with similar goals to meet, chart their progress, and discuss problems. Those who want to lose weight can form a mini

Weight Watchers' Club; those who want to improve their basketball skills can become the "NBA or Bust" team, and so on. They will need guidance at first, but eventually each support group can take on a life of its own.

SHARED LEVEL III GOALS

When using individualized instruction strategies such as task cards or contracts, students can work in pairs or small groups to urge each other on and give each other feedback. This strategy is somewhat easier to implement than the support group idea described above and can be accomplished either with or without formal support groups.

SMALL GROUP COOPERATION

Students can be placed in small groups for a cooperative task to be accomplished by each group independently. For example, each group could be required to keep a soccer ball in the air until it is headed 25 times including at least three times by each group member. When a group completes the task, group members can then coach and cheer other groups. Clear directions may be needed for this kind of support to occur.

CHEATER TEST

I've given a cheater test over concepts covered in class such as weight control, the overload principle, and so on. On a cheater test, students are encouraged to give answers to students who need them. Betting them that no one will get a perfect paper even by "cheating" sometimes escalates their efforts.

VOLUNTARY GROUPING

Allowing students to voluntarily group themselves (except when equal groups are required) permits students to form groups that they perceive to be most supportive. I've found that as kids get more comfortable and as they interact more and more with Level IV, groups become more heterogeneous.

RECIPROCAL TEACHING

Reciprocal teaching (Mosston, 1981) is particularly useful if the kind of feedback that partners give to each other is carefully structured. Armed with three or four cues that describe proper form concerning the skill to be practiced, one partner watches the other perform and then shares one or more things that the other has done correctly. No corrective comments are allowed until students learn to give "positives." Then, one positive can be followed by one "needs work" or what George Graham calls a "not yet." The structure can be gradually loosened as students learn how to give feedback. I've tried reciprocal teaching with Kim Weaver's class of 20 emotionally handicapped and disruptive boys ages 7 to 11 and it went surprisingly well. One little guy asked me "What if they do everything right?" "Tell him," I said, so he yelled over his shoulder, "You did everything right!" Based on Mosston's idea, Bob Blanchette makes a big deal of this strategy with his middle-school kids by calling those who help "little Ts" and himself the "big T" (for little and big Teacher). Peter Teppler has systematized reciprocal teaching in a swimming unit required of all students at his high school. He instructs students in the different kinds of feedback (i.e., positive, negative, general, specific) and how to effectively give feedback. They receive written instructions and pictures to aid them in teaching, as the following excerpt shows (with some hypothetical student responses):

Unit Information Sheet

Teacher: P. Teppler

Course: PE 30

Unit: Swimming/CARING

Length of Unit: 2 weeks (6 lessons)

Percentage of Course:

Objectives:
1. The student will attend a minimum of 4 of the 6 classes.

2. The student will be able to demonstrate a knowledge of stroke and skill mechanics on a written exam.

3. The student will assist a partner in perfecting or improving his/her swimming skills.

4. The student will receive assistance in improving his/her own swimming skills from a partner.

5. The student will complete a check sheet for each of the instructional lessons.

Learning Activities:

The teacher is a last resource only. Information is obtained in the following order:

a. sequenced picture

b. task description sheets

c. information from your partner

d. the teacher

Evaluation:
1. Attendance is worth 25%. You must attend a minimum of 4 classes or you will lose the unit.

2. Written quiz: on stroke mechanics worth 25%.

3. Self-evaluation as a swimmer. This is your SKILL LEVEL and is worth 25% of the unit.

4. A confidential evaluation of you by your partner as a *teacher*, worth 25% of the unit. This is *not* of you as a swimmer.

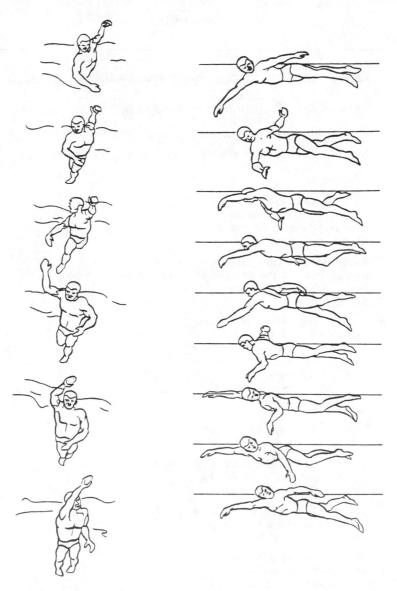

FRONT CRAWL STROKE: front view   FRONT CRAWL STROKE: side view.
from below the line of travel.

Swimming

Your Name: _____   Your Partner's Name: _____

Lesson #1   Skill: "Crawl Stroke" or "Front Crawl"

Drills & Progression	*Partner's Comment*
1. Swim 4 lengths. Partner looks for arm entering in front of the shoulder.	First 2 lengths: good! Last 2: a little sloppy.
2. Swim 2 lengths. Swimmer concentrates on pulling directly backward with the power almost parallel to the direction of travel.	Looked OK
3. Swim 4 lengths and have your partner check for maximum elbow flexion when power hand is at shoulder level.	Could be higher. Again, first 2 lengths were better.
4. Swim 4 lengths and have your partner check that your recovery starts before the elbow is fully extended. Palm never presses upward towards the surface.	Nope. Needs work.
5. Swim 2 lengths using a pull directly down the midline.	OK
6. Swim 2 lengths using a pull below your shoulders.	OK
7. Swim 2 lengths using a pull that is somewhat "S" shaped. Pull "out-in-out" along the stroke.	Needs work.
8. Tell your partner to record which of the 3 pulls feels best for you: mid-line, shoulder, or "S".	Mid-line
9. Swim 2 lengths and have your partner check to see if your arms are "phased." That is, one arm begins to pull as the other begins its recovery.	Pretty good.
10. Swim 2 lengths and have your partner check to see that you are rolling your upper body. That means *not* keeping your chest parallel with the bottom of the pool. Roll towards the arm that is pulling.	Not much roll.

Swimming (Cont.)

Drills & Progression	*Partner's Comment*
11. Tell your partner that the flutter kick provides very little forward propulsion but serves primarily to balance and stabilize the rolling swimmer.	✔
12. Swim 2 lengths and concentrate on originating the kick from the hips.	Mostly from knees.
13. Swim 2 lengths concentrating on: 1) pointing your toes backwards behind you; 2) turning your toes in (pigeon-toed).	#1 OK #2 No
14. Swim 2 lengths, concentrating on using only a very shallow (18") kick.	✔
15. Swim 2 lengths, concentrating on never breaking the surface of the water with your feet at any time.	✔
16. Swim one length breathing in by turning your head to the left side only while your right arm is entering the water.	A struggle.
17. Swim one length breathing in by turning your head to the right side only while your left arm is entering the water.	Seemed smoother.
18. Tell your partner which side is more comfortable to breathe on and have him/her record it.	✔
19. Swim 2 lengths and concentrate on exhaling completely when your face is still in the water.	OK
20. Swim 2 lengths and try breathing only on every second cycle of the arms. That is once every 4 pulls of the arms.	Not quite.
21. Tell your partner how this compares with breathing on each and every cycle of the arms. Have your partner record which one you prefer.	Breathing every time (so far).

CROSS-AGE TEACHING

Cross-age teaching gives students more responsibility for helping others. Cross-age teaching isn't a new idea, but one experience with it convinced me of its potential as a Level IV activity. Connie Word and I developed and took turns teaching a
3-week Teaching Self-Defense unit to 20 teenagers in an alternative (diversion) school. Those who attended regularly and
demonstrated some minimal ability to teach the skills we had
presented qualified to teach two self-defense lessons to fifth
graders. Seven of the 20 met the criteria; one of the seven did
not feel confident enough to teach but did volunteer to drive and
observe. The other six divided into two teams, and each team
taught two 30-minute lessons to 15 to 20 fifth graders on suc-
cessive days. During the drive over they were grimly silent, a rare
treat for me as one of the drivers; I could almost hear them sweat.
But once they started teaching, both their fears and mine disap-
peared. I think they were better teachers than Connie or me, and
they were certainly better than some physical education majors
I've observed! The lessons were partly fitness oriented, and they
remembered to tell their students the reasons for doing each exercise, what muscles were involved, and so on.

One kid presented a couple of discipline problems—something
we hadn't talked about. The first time, David walked over to this
kid who was probably a lot like he was at that age and used a
line that I had used on him a week earlier! That held him until
the second day when Colleen called the same kid out in front of
the group to demonstrate, knocked him on his butt, and then
calmly pointed out that if he would have widened his base of support as she had taught them he would still be standing. He got
the message. The best part of this experience was the discussion
afterward. They had to have a smoke break, of course, but all
the talk was of going around the city teaching self-defense to fifth
graders ("Yeah, fifth graders are just right. Fourth graders are
too young and sixth graders too old."). They were on to
something else the next day, but at least they glimpsed the ex-
citement of helping people they didn't know, of feeling responsible for a little piece of the education of others. After I shared this
experience with some teachers, one of them, Terry Cooper, tried
it with some of her more troublesome sixth graders. She asked
them to help teach her first graders; they were great teachers!

TEACHING ASSISTANTS

A teaching assistant's program can be useful if structured to make a contribution to the development of caring attitudes and behaviors. Three guidelines have helped me: (1) Require some criteria for becoming a teaching assistant based on demonstrated helping qualities rather than on athletic ability; (2) give teaching assistants real helping roles rather than the usual towel handout or calisthenic leadership type responsibilities; (3) create a teaching assistant program within the class rather than from outside the class. Regarding this last point, peer teaching can work if students know ahead of time the criteria required to become a teaching assistant, are convinced of the validity of the criteria, and believe that the selection process is fair.

SPOTTING

Requirements for spotting can also be turned into a Level IV activity by teaching and emphasizing this helping role.

COMMUNITY PROJECTS

Community projects can be useful in emphasizing the importance of caring as a major purpose in life. Some examples are cross-age teaching, helping with the Special Olympics, teaching the elderly basic exercises or self-defense skills, running laps to raise money for charity, helping to teach CPR, and assisting in community recreation programs. One specific example is Stanley Sajecki's Xaverian High School Tumbling Team in Brooklyn, New York. The team is organized as a club and performs 10 to 15 times a year in hospitals, homes for the elderly, and schools for the handicapped. Of course, the teacher must commit considerable energy to making contracts, travel arrangements, and so on to get such projects started. Too often when such projects are attempted, students are not sufficiently prepared for the experience and, importantly, few if any criteria are required for participation. A training program ought to precede any such venture, and students should earn the privilege of participating by meeting specific criteria. Student sharing can be used to involve students in developing the criteria.

CURRICULUM CONSIDERATIONS

There are two approaches to inserting Level IV into the curriculum. One is to "sneak" it without disturbing the curriculum itself. For example, reciprocal teaching can be used to teach a scheduled activity, teachable moments can be used to point out Level IV behaviors, kids who demonstrate caring can be reinforced, and scheduled activities can be modified once in a while so that they are more cooperative in nature.

A second approach is to alter the structure of the curriculum to accommodate Level IV more visibly and formally. For example, one day each week could be designated as Level IV day, either as part of the scheduled activity or free from the restrictions of the scheduled activity. This would force you to do something related to Level IV every week. A planned community project would also require a change in the curriculum. So would regularly planned student sharing, especially if such planning led to changes in curriculum. Both approaches have merit. Changing the curriculum will ensure that you do something, but much can be accomplished without curriculum revision.

INDIVIDUALIZATION

Research (Johnson et al., 1981; Johnson & Johnson, 1978) suggests that cooperative activities promote achievement, productivity, and interpersonal relations more effectively than either competitive or individualistic activities. However, these studies mask individual differences. That is, while more kids might learn better by cooperative methods, some learn better with self-paced instructional materials and others are motivated by competition. Caring is presented here as an important quality for students (and teachers), but not necessarily as the most effective approach to learning. That depends on the individual student.

A number of factors influence the development of caring in any individual (Hogan, 1973). Some students come to your program with considerable exposure to these factors, others with less or little. Therefore, as with the other levels, some students will need more help than others in order to develop positive caring experiences. Since Caring is a Level IV activity, students who have lots of needs and/or a confused or uncomfortable sense of identity may not be able to care about others very much or very often until their own needs have been met. Again, your teaching style, setting, and students will influence the kinds of interaction strategies that seem most appropriate to you.

CONCLUSION

Functioning at Level IV, Caring, contributes to social stability at a time in our history when relationships appear to be more transient, people more mobile, and the search for self more pronounced. Reaching out—not only because we need people to support us but because we want to be of service to others—is a value of high priority and one which may first require some measure of self-control, involvement, and self-responsibility. This chapter has described strategies and implementation ideas to better acquaint students with Level IV. You need to decide for yourself how many and what kind of Level IV activities to introduce in your gym.

CHAPTER 7

GOING BEYOND
THE LEVELS

Levels I through IV provide a framework for working and playing in the gym and in life. Some students and teachers who decide to adopt them see them as being etched in stone. The history of the levels has not been so clear-cut, however. They have undergone countless revisions and will no doubt continue to be reworked as long as we continue to experience problems with their application and to dream up new angles. Teachers who have been attracted to the levels have not only adopted them but have freely modified them as well. Oregon Governor Victor Atiyeh's Physical Education Leadership Training Project for High Risk Youth (1981-83) provided an opportunity for the most extensive overhaul of the levels to date. After studying the levels and interaction strategies and field-testing them with mostly "problem" kids, the project staff then evaluated these levels and strategies, as well as the whole process they had experienced. Several changes resulted from this procedure.

NEEDS AND VALUES

The "etched in stone" implication has always bothered me, because I am influenced by the philosophy of such scholars as Paulo Friere (1970, 1974) and Carl Rogers (1983). Friere's philosophy in particular raises questions about teaching a specific framework of values to students. Friere emphasizes people's capacity to reflect and act and is highly critical of the "oppressive pedagogy" of teacher prescriptions and student compliance which dominate the educational process. He favors a "problem posing" approach in which both teacher and students identify the problems and engage in trying to solve them. As a result, everyone becomes involved in the process of either renewing and modifying present cultural values or creating new values appropriate to present needs.

Although many view Friere's ideas as radical, educators in recent years have argued for a more process-oriented education. For example, Mathis (1977) argues that our educational tradition is primarily amoral because it fails to engage students in questioning the demands of our culture but rather emphasizes the how and where of performance.

> The examination of such issues as morality, the good life, and self-identity are not encouraged by a system of education that deemphasizes a concern for the process of learning. . . To have a moral education is not only to be guided toward the internalization of a system of ethics; it is also to benefit from a process that is itself. . .capable of being analyzed but always demanding further analysis. (Mathis, 1977, pp. 202-203)

Friere's problem-posing has been tried in physical education (MacKay, 1978), but I found that the strength of both the socialization process and the need for approval among the kids with whom I've worked over the years prevented free-wheeling, process-oriented problem-posing sessions. To prevent total chaos, I needed structure in the form of specific goals and strategies. Within that structure I tried to build in gradual responsibility for the students' own intentions and behaviors to capture at least some of Friere's and Rogers' image of the person as a reflecting-acting being. However, student responsibility did not extend to examining the underlying values of this structure.

INTERACTION STRATEGIES

I'm not sure how to do this. The closest I've come is with my Governor's Project Staff and in teacher workshops. One time I overheard one of my high school students tell one of his pals about the levels: "I know it don't make no sense but that's what he wants to hear." What did I do about it? I got depressed, then went to my thinking room and dreamed up a new version of the levels. . .without further consultation with my students!

TEACHER TALK

Teacher talk provides an opportunity to gently point out the tentativeness of the levels. Can everything be neatly labeled and categorized? Does life really work this way? If changes have been made in the program, share the changes and perhaps the reasons. All of this can be done with one-liners and/or in brief sessions at the beginning or end of class. The point is to balance class rules and the need for a framework with an attitude which reflects receptivity to change so that nothing is perceived as etched in stone.

Dialog can also help. Encourage students to express their views; ask them questions rather than always giving answers.

Students may believe, for example, that survival of the fittest makes more sense than respecting others' rights and helping. Encourage them to talk about it and to give evidence to support their view.

REFLECTION TIME/STUDENT SHARING

Asking students to reflect on the usefulness and effectiveness of the levels and requesting modifications will also help them to go beyond the levels. Reflection time strategies and brief student sharing sessions can be used to accomplish this. At the end of each grading period, Frank O'Toole has his middle-school Level III students give him what they like best and least about his approach to teaching physical education.

A VALIDATION COMMITTEE

Establishing a committee of students in charge of validating or modifying the levels and strategies so that they are more effective for everyone would mark a shift in emphasis from "What's good for me" to "What's good for everyone." Some criteria would be necessary for committee membership; perhaps the best qualification might be demonstrated success at all four levels (to be spelled out more specifically by the teacher and perhaps eventually by students). If the whole class eventually qualifies, they could operate as a committee of the whole. How much time should be devoted to committee meetings and related details would need to be worked out.

The teacher's role would also need to be delineated. He/she may want to hold veto power at first, perhaps working his/her way into the role of facilitator and eventually onto the sidelines. The committee's agenda would be to carefully evaluate the levels and strategies for strengths and weaknesses and to suggest additions, deletions, and modifications. The levels, strategies, reinforcement system, grading policy—everything—would be open to change. The teacher may need to set the agenda at first, taking into consideration the levels as a whole and then each level individually, along with the strategies being used.

Jonathan Kozol (1972) has reminded those who desire to open their own school that democratic decision-making at the top sometimes ends up changing the philosophy that provided the impetus for opening the school in the first place! Yet if Friere, Rogers, and Mathis are right, students need to learn to make these very fundamental decisions. The key to going beyond is to help students evaluate and recommend changes in the values which underly the levels and strategies. The actual implementation is up to the teachers. If things aren't working very effectively and student ideas seem to help, immediate implementation may be warranted. Otherwise, planning effectively for the next year might be the best way to proceed.

CURRICULUM CONSIDERATIONS AND INDIVIDUALIZATION

A sense of going beyond should be integrated slowly as one of your interaction strategies only if you see it as something that you want to implement. I myself haven't had much experience with the implementation of this concept, and even teachers who believe in the four levels often balk at this motion when I introduce it. They apparently don't want to let go of a value system that they believe in. The guideline is to go slowly with the goal of giving students some experience in program evaluation and change.

Individual students will be capable of and receptive to *going beyond* depending on a myriad of factors. Perhaps the biggest problem lies in helping students move from self (i.e., "What's in it for me?") to others ("What's good for everybody?"). Obviously, some experience with Level IV would help students to make this transition.

CHAPTER 8

THE PROBLEM
OF BEING
HUMAN: SOME
CLOSING THOUGHTS

I love country music! The songs tell stories of happiness and sadness, of new loves and lost loves, of getting drunk for right reasons and wrong reasons, of winning and losing the struggles to survive—in short, country music talks about being human. This book has presented some goals and strategies for your consideration; perhaps we could call this approach an alternative model for teaching physical education and coaching organized sport. Throughout the first seven chapters the model has referred to teachers and coaches who have pioneered some of the strategies, and to my own struggles. In this sense, it is certainly human. But does the model really capture the kind of humanness that country music portrays? Let's examine the major themes of the model to determine this.

HUMANNESS AND THIS MODEL

1. The model has five goals: self-control, involvement, self-responsibility, caring, and going beyond (to evaluate and change the program and its underlying values).

2. The goals attempt to meet disciplinary and motivational program needs based upon an analysis of current trends.

3. The goals are presented as developmental levels in the sense that each level builds upon the preceding one, although they can be, and often are, taught at the same time.

4. The levels emphasize student responsibility for the following areas: being under control, being involved, selecting and carrying out personal choices, reaching out to others, and evaluating and changing the model in line with current needs.

5. Value transfer is essential to making the model work, because the levels represent values that are important in life.

6. The model includes a wide selection of strategies which emphasize student interaction with the levels in order to make them viable choices in the students' lives.

7. Several curriculum options are available for implementing the model. Selection depends upon specific program needs, students in the program, and the teacher's style.

8. The teacher must take individual student needs into consideration in order to effectively implement the model.

In reading these themes, you may have the feeling, as I do, that the humanness of the model falls a bit short. Remarks throughout the book underscore the individuality of both students and teachers, the importance of the student-teacher relationship, the need for a sense of humor, and the very real possibility that any strategy could backfire in its implementation. I have deliberately minimized direct references to you, the reader, using myself or other teachers and coaches in the strategy descriptions in order to reduce the possibility that you would perceive the strategies to be prescriptions for a great program rather than options that need to be carefully selected, adapted and implemented. Still, models often are interpreted as prescriptions that ought to be applied without the many reservations and modifications that our individuality demands. In this closing chapter I want to further emphasize the humanness of this model.

VALUES

Let's start with the goals of the model which are the levels. These levels—self-control, self-responsibility, involvement, caring, are in reality values. I have tried to give some theoretical support for these values by briefly analyzing current trends in our society, referring to historical values, and describing resultant program needs. I could have expanded on this framework by tracing the concept of self-control back to Rousseau, Kant, John Stuart Mill, David Hume, and others and by doing the same for the other levels. However, theoretical support for my values has been kept brief, not only to retain the focus on program implementation but also because no amount of support can fully justify anyone's values. My values are just that: something I value. They remain outside the grasp of science (Junnell, 1979, p. 7), no matter what evidence I muster on their behalf. As I said at the outset, my values come from my experiences, my observations, and my reflective thoughts regarding these experiences and observations. Both historical and current trends do provide some objective support which might be useful in developing a rationale for principals, school boards, and organized sport administrators, but such support is neither sufficient nor the real reason for my value selection.

TEACHERS AND STUDENTS

As mentioned above, this model attempts to account for the humanness of students, teachers, and coaches. However, being human makes the practical transformation of the model in the gyms and on the playing fields impossible to fully detail. For example, the model requires teachers to be confident enough in their abilities to be open to incorporating parts of the model in their programs if it makes sense to do so, vulnerable enough to share problems with students, reflective enough to analyze their own style, setting, and students, and creative enough to modify and change the model as needed. This is quite a large order for those of us who are merely human! The model takes into account the individuality of students, but motivation can't be packaged as neatly as the levels suggest. Kids who feel insecure will behave in self-controlled ways because they are afraid to be assertive, will have trouble setting goals that are different from those of their friends, and may care for others because they need caring in return. Kids who are confident will try new skills and practice old skills because they have confidence in the outcomes. Kids who are raised in the street may find that self-control and caring conflict with the "survival of the fittest" street ethic. Kids who are always on the receiving end of Level IV help may feel worse

than if they were left alone. Kids who fail most of the time won't be very open to Level II involvement. Kids labeled "bad" may resist interaction with the levels because they fear losing status with friends, may think they will be expected to continue improving, and might lose an old identity without gaining an adequate replacement. And so on. If kids weren't human, implementation would be so much easier (but so much more boring)!

EVALUATION OF THE MODEL

Values can be debated and, as we have seen, theoretical support can provide some assistance in developing one's argument. However, an evaluation of the values underlying the model can only be taken so far; beyond that, personal or district-wide biases about what ought to be taught take over. I have shared my values and some theoretical support as the basis for this model, and I pointed out in the preface as well as in this closing chapter that these values have come out of my own experiences and thoughts. It follows that your evaluation of the values underlying the model must remain personal. You need only be open to new ideas, not swallow them whole.

The strategies and curriculum ideas are another matter. In the preface, I said that only those strategies which worked somewhere would be included. By that I simply meant if a teacher or coach reported to me that a particular strategy helped students interact with a particular level, I included it. Are their—and my—subjective judgments enough? This is a more complex question than it first appears. I have been encouraged by respected colleagues to collect data in order to better determine the effectiveness of the strategies for helping students with self-control, involvement, self-responsibility, and caring. And I have done so on a couple of occasions, most notably using a number of subjective and objective procedures with a group of students over the period of a year (Hellison, 1978, pp. 49-65). Taken together, these procedures showed some changes, although no controls were used and more positive changes were found using subjective procedures. Some colleagues have suggested a longitudinal study, with controls, to check for changes outside the gym over a period of time. They seem to feel that interviews with former students would shed some light on what stuck and what didn't. I have been content, perhaps more accurately committed, to

> fully participate in the process as it unfolds. Through the years, I have simply reported my biases, intentions, and experiences as I perceived them, including setting, students, goals, strategies, whatever data were gathered, and my impressions without trying to generalize beyond these specific experiences. (Hellison, 1983, p. 103)

The only modification of this approach has been to include the subjective judgments of other teachers and coaches in my recent findings. My approach is in line with William James' argument that we can only know truth by experiencing it, that our own conscious experiences are valid data (McDonagh, 1973, pp. 50-51). However, traditional research procedures might help clarify what works, especially if some of the newer research methodologies were to be employed. For example, Anderson suggests analyzing past records to determine the effectiveness of teaching responsibility in physical education (Anderson, 1980, pp. 102-103). I'm not very interested, primarily because my style—and identity—is better suited to what I am now doing. I also feel that using these strategies, especially with high-risk youth, will mostly lead to subtle and minimal value transfer unless reinforced by significant others. However, it would clearly be valuable, from my point of view, to check the extent of student interaction with the levels. How much class or practice time is spent modeling, discussing, experiencing, reinforcing, and reflecting upon the levels? This wouldn't tell us whether kids were becoming more controlled, involved, responsible, and so on, but it would show whether our goals were being implemented, whether students were truly interacting with our values.

Focusing on the process rather than the product doesn't mean that the model isn't worth doing. It only means that we are swimming upstream at this point. If we continue to do so, perhaps others both in and outside of physical education and sport will follow suit. This might lead to significant changes as more students perceive self-control, involvement, self-responsibility, and caring as viable options in their lives.

IMPROVING SCHOOLS

Schools were identified in the first chapter as having a confused mission, being unsuccessful at efforts at inclusion, and suffering from specialization and fragmentation because of size. Let's return to those issues here in the last chapter. Implementation of the proposed model in physical education, organized sport, or both, would address these concerns. The model reflects a clear set of values and the principle of inclusion of all students within a progressive set of guidelines. It advocates a group feeling based on student ownership and emphasizes caring and concern for others. Whether schools are influenced by the model depends once again on a variety of human factors; "bottom-up" change when initiated by a single teacher working alone to implement the model is certainly sloppier than the kind of "top-down" change mandated by school leadership. However, William James pointed out the humanness of bottom-up change when he wrote:

I am done with the great things and big things. . .I am for
those tiny, invisible, molecular moral forces that work from
individual to individual, creeping through the crannies of the
world. . .which, if you give them time, will rend the hardest
monuments of man's pride. (James, 1920)

WHAT'S WORTH DOING

I always come back to the same two questions: What's worth doing? and, Is it working? For all of us, certain values are worth
trying to put into practice; others don't matter so much. The
values that form the basis for this book matter more than other
values to me, both for kids who seem headed for nonproductive
or counterproductive roles in our society and for those who seem
likely to be the future leaders of education, government, science,
and industry. The struggle to put these values into practice for
myself and my students is high human drama, and when I go
to sleep at night, it is this trying that seems to count the most.
But is it working? That is, does all this trying lead anywhere?

I've already pointed out that any evaluation of the model that
focuses on value transfer in student lives may not show significant results, and that programs are most likely to change in the
direction of the model by gradual person-to-person modeling and
communication. Ernest Becker (1973) argues that the overriding
question is what's worth doing, not whether it is working. According to Becker, most of us need a heroic myth to get through
life. Working at something worth doing is essential to that heroic
myth. So is the recognition that our heroism is largely mythical;
it's the trying that counts.

> What we are describing is not a creature who . . .transforms
> the world . . .in some miraculous ways, but rather a creature
> who takes more of the world into himself and develops new
> forms of courage and endurance. (Becker, 1973, p. 279)

> The most one can hope to achieve is a certain relatedness,
> an openness to experience that makes him less of a driven
> burden on others. (Becker, 1973, p. 259)

> We can't imagine that the world will be any pleasanter or
> less tragic a place. . .Men are doomed to live in an overwhelm-
> ingly tragic and demonic world. (Becker, 1973, p. 281)

If Becker is right, the question becomes whether the model presented in this book helps to answer what's worth doing for you. If it does, it's yours to try. You might even change the world a click or two in the process, despite Becker's pessimism! As for me, I'll struggle on with the model, but I'll keep playing country music too, to remind me of the humanness of the world. . .and myself.

REFERENCES

AAHPER. (1976). *Personalized learning in physical education*. Washington: AAHPER.

Alschuler, A.S. (1980). *School discipline: A socially literate solution*. New York: McGraw Hill.

Anderson, W.G. (1980). *Analysis of teaching physical education*. St. Louis: Mosby.

Basic Stuff Series. (1981). Reston, VA: AAHPERD.

Becker, E. (1973). *The denial of death*. New York: Free Press.

Bronfenbrenner, U. (1980, Dec.). On making human beings human. *Character*, **2**, 1-7.

Brophy, J., & Evertson, C. (1976). *Learning from teaching*. Boston: Allyn & Bacon.

Cody, K. (1976, May). Must competitive sport for youth be all wins and losses? *Keynote*, p. 9.

Corbin, C.B., & Lindsey, R. (1983). *Fitness for life* (2nd ed.). Glenview, IL: Scott, Forsman & Co.

Cox, H. (1979). *Turning east: The promise and peril of the new Orientalism*. New York: Touchstone Books.

Craig, D. (1982, Dec.). What values? *Ethics in education*. **2**.

Darst, P.W., & Armstrong, G.P. (1980). *Outdoor adventure activities for school and recreation programs.* Minneapolis: Burgess.

de Charms, R. (1976). *Enhancing motivation: Change in the classroom.* New York: Irvington.

de Charms, R. (1979). Personal causation and perceived control. In L.C. Perlmutter & R.A. Monty (Eds.), *Choice and perceived control.* Hillsdale, NJ: Erlbaum.

Friere, P. (1970). *Pedagogy of the oppressed.* New York: The Seabury Press.

Friere, P. (1974). *Education for critical consciousness.* New York: The Seabury Press.

Glasser, W. (1965). Reality therapy. New York: Harper & Row.

Guthrie, G. (1982). *Be your own coach.* Portland: ASIEP.

Harris, J.C., Blankenship, K., Cawley, M.E., Crouse, K.R., Smith, M.D., & Winfrey, W.A. (1982, April). Ethical behavior and victory in sport: Value systems at play. *JOPERD,* **53**, 37ff.

Hellison, D. (1978). *Beyond balls and bats: Alienated (and other) youth in the gym.* Washington: AAHPER.

Hellison, D. (1983, April). The magnificent seven. *JOPERD,* **54**, 60-61.

Hellison, D. (1983). It only takes one case to prove a possibility . . .and beyond. In T.J. Templin & J.K. Olson (Eds.), *Teaching in physical education.* Champaign, IL: Human Kinetics.

Hogan, R. (1973). Moral conduct and moral character: A psychological perspective. *Psychological bulletin,* **79**, 217-232.

Horrocks, R.N. (1978, Sept.). Resolving conflict in the gymnasium. *JOPERD,* **49**, 61.

James, W. (1920). In James, H. (Ed.), *Source letters of William James.* Volume II. Boston: Atlantic Monthly Press.

Johnson, D.W. (1980). Constructive peer relationships, social development, and cooperative learning experiences: Implications for the prevention of drug abuse. *Journal of Drug Education,* **10**, 7-24.

Johnson, D.W., & Johnson, R.T. (1978). Cooperative, competitive, and individualistic learning. *Journal of Research and Development in Education,* **12**, 3-15.

Johnson, D.W., Maruyama, G., Johnson, R., Nelson, D., & Skon, L. (1981, Jan.). The effects of cooperative, competitive, and individualistic goal structures on achievement: A meta-analysis. *Psychological Bulletin*, **89**, 47-62.

Jones, V.F., & Jones, L.S. (1981). *Responsible classroom discipline*. Boston: Allyn & Bacon.

Junnell, J.S. (1979). *Matters of feeling: Values education reconsidered*. Delta Kappa Educational Foundation.

Jurkovic, G.J., & Selman, R.L. (1980). A developmental analysis of intrapsychic understanding: Treating emotional disturbances in children. In R.L. Selman & R. Yando (Eds.), *New directions for child development*. San Francisco: Jossey-Bass.

Kozol, J. (1972). *Free schools*. Boston: Houghton Mifflin.

Lambdin, D. (1976). Quiet individualizing: What one teacher did. In AAHPER, *Personalized learning in physical education*. Washington: AAHPER.

Lickona, T. (1982, Sept.). Fostering moral community. *Ethics Education*, **2**.

Locke, L.F., & Higgins, S. (1976, Oct.). Review of physical education instructional techniques. JOPER, **47**, 76-77.

Lyon, H.C. Jr. (1971). *Learning to feel—Feeling to learn*. Columbus: Charles E. Merrill.

MacKay, R. (1978). *Whose body? Whose mind? The implications of Paulo Friere's problem posing method for a humanistic approach to an active health program*. (Unpublished master's thesis, University of British Columbia.)

Martens, R. (1978). *Joy and sadness in children's sports*. Champaign, IL: Human Kinetics.

Maslow, A.H. (1970). *Motivation and personality* (2nd ed.). New York: Harper & Row.

Mathis, B.C. (1977). To train or to educate: A moral decision. In L.F. Stiles & B.D. Johnson (Eds.), *Morality examined: Guidelines for teachers*. Princeton, NJ: Princeton Book Co.

McDonagh, J. (1973). The open-ended psychology of William James. *Journal of Humanistic Psychology*, **13**, 49-54.

McNeill, J.L. (1982). Moral education and the community of commitment. *Canadian Journal of Education*, **7**, 34-45.

Morgan, W.P. (1979, Feb.). Negative addiction in runners. *The Physician and Sportsmedicine,* **7**, 57-70.

Morris, D., & Stiehl, J. (in press). *Physical education: From intent to action.* Columbus: Charles E. Merrill.

Mosston, M. (1981). *Teaching physical education* (2nd ed.). Columbus: Charles E. Merrill.

Orlick, T.D. (1978). *The cooperative sports and games book.* New York: Pantheon Books.

Orlick, T.D. (1980). *In pursuit of excellence.* Champaign, IL: Human Kinetics.

Pangrazi, R. (1982, Nov.-Dec.). Physical education, self-concept, and achievement. *JOPERD,* **53**, 16-18.

Raffini, J.P. (1980). *Discipline: negotiating conflicts with today's kids.* Englewood Cliffs, NJ: Prentice-Hall.

Roberts, G.C. (1977). Children in competition: Assignment of responsibility for winning and losing. *Proceedings of the NCPEAM/NAPECW National Conference,* pp. 328-340.

Rogers, C.R. (1983). *Freedom to learn for the 80's.* Columbus: Charles E. Merrill.

Rohnke, K. (1977). *Cowstails and cobras.* Hamilton, MA: Project Adventure.

Sheehy, G. (1981). *Pathfinders.* New York: Morrow & Co.

Shepro, D., & Knuttgen, H.G. (1979). *Complete conditioning: The no-nonsense guide to fitness and good health.* Reading, MA: Addison-Wesley.

Turner, L.F., & Turner, S.L. (1976). *Elementary physical education: More than just games.* Palo Alto, CA: Peek Publications.

Wolfgang, C.H., & Glickman, C.D. (1980). *Solving discipline problems: Strategies for classroom teachers.* Boston: Allyn & Bacon.

Yiannakis, A. (1980). Sport and deviancy: A review and appraisal. *Motor Skills: Theory into Practice,* **4**, 59-64.

INDEX
